Turbo Pascal

Turbo Pascal

Procedures and Functions for IBM PCs and Compatibles

Patrick Philippot
IBM, France

Translated and edited by
David Beeson
and
Seth Keith

JOHN WILEY & SONS
Chichester • New York • Brisbane • Toronto • Singapore

This is a translation from the French book by
Patrick Philippot: *TURBO PASCAL, Procédures et fonctions pour IBM PC et compatibles*
published by Editions EYROLLES, Paris.

British Library Cataloguing in Publication Data:

Philipott, P.
TURBO PASCAL : procedures and functions
for IBM PCs and compatibles.
1. IBM Personal Computer—Programming
2. Turbo Pascal (Computer program)
I. Title
005.2'65 QA76.8.I2594

ISBN 0 471 91632 3

Printed and bound in Great Britain by Anchor Brendon Ltd, Tiptree, Essex

Contents

Introduction

1 WHY TURBO PASCAL?

The arrival of Turbo Pascal on the market for high level languages quite rightly created a stir. Contrary to what one might expect, this is not another Pascal compiler but the implementation of a wholly new concept of a development environment for personal or professional software.

A level of interactivity nearly equivalent to that of a BASIC interpreter together with fast compilation and execution as well as extensive memory access facilities, are a series of advantages programmers will not want to do without once they have tried them.

No compiler has ever provided such ease of use or such performance levels. This product, through its unique qualities and its low cost, will overcome any lingering hesitation amongst those who have not yet dared try Pascal.

The immediate success of this software provided the most striking proof of its worth, and we believe there is more yet in store.

2 WHY THE IBM PC?

Though the IBM PC has never claimed to be the most advanced machine in its class, from a hardware point of view, it does have a number of advantages.

First of all, because it has become something of a standard, it can take advantage of all sorts of developments, both in hardware and in software, to say nothing of the tempting offers made by various companies which tend to focus a great deal of their activity on this machine.

Moreover, and this is certainly the most important point for those involved in software development, the IBM PC is fully documented at both the hardware and operating system levels. Everything has been said or written about the PC, as the outpouring of journals and books on this computer makes entirely clear.

This machine therefore provides a reliable and solid work base.

3 TURBO PASCAL ON THE IBM PC

The meeting of these two stars was bound to awaken the enthusiasm of dedicated programmers such as ourselves. The possibility offered by Turbo Pascal of accessing system resources directly is almost unique in high level languages. The flexibility provided in PC programming makes it possible to design almost any type of application on this machine in Turbo Pascal, reducing to a minimum the need to resort to the dubious joys (for amateurs or programmers in a hurry) of assembly language.

4 WHY PUBLISH A COLLECTION OF ROUTINES IN TURBO PASCAL?

Someone meeting the Turbo Pascal instruction set for the first time may be surprised by how relatively few in number they are, compared to the sometimes terrifying numbers facing beginners using a BASIC interpreter.

This is to leave out of account the extraordinary construction possibilities represented by Pascal in general and by Turbo Pascal in particular.

Programmers can build up their own libraries of procedures and functions as their experience of the language grows. There will, however, be those who are uneasy in their work on applications because of their unfamiliarity with certain mechanisms. Sometimes, it will be lack of time which prevents their developing a routine which could provide the services required.

We felt it would be of little value simply to modify the Turbo Pascal manual, as the manual is very good. Our approach was to suggest a procedure and function library drawn from the most effective possible use of system resources which are not highlighted, or may even be ignored, by standard Turbo Pascal procedures.

The procedures and functions proposed are not simply examples, but can be used directly, as new instructions, in your programs.

In the course of this book we shall look at screen windows, graphics, floppy disk and keyboard management, and much else.

The procedures and functions proposed here go from the simplest (a few instructions or even just one instruction) to a level of complexity which we hope we always manage to keep within the bounds of what is strictly necessary. In most cases they will provide a convenient and modular extension to the basic language.

Happy programming!

Preliminaries

1 OPERATING INSTRUCTIONS

Throughout this book we shall assume the reader is familiar with the basic operations of Turbo Pascal. We shall also assume that the reader has the minimum knowledge needed to make use of the system.

All the routines proposed will work under the following conditions:

—the hardware is an IBM PC/XT or a 100% compatible machine (see below),
—the operating system is PC-DOS,
—for video or graphics routines, an IBM monochrome or standard graphics board, or some similar board, is available,
—if version 3.0 of Turbo Pascal is required, the fact will be drawn to the readers' attention.

These routines have all been tested but there may be difficulties in particular conditions. If this occurs, write to us, care of the publisher, stating the details of your problem. We shall do all we can to solve it. Please do not hesitate to suggest possible improvements for later editions.

In keeping with the general marketing philosophy of Turbo Pascal, no restrictions are placed on the use of these procedures for your own programs even if you intend to market them commercially. All that we ask is that if the book has been useful to you, make sure those around you know....

2 COMPATIBILITY

When it comes to the issue of compatibility between these routines and non-IBM hardware, the following needs to be clearly stated:

—hardware is regarded as being compatible with an IBM PC if a program that strictly respects DOS conventions can run without difficulty on it.

This means that in general all the routines proposed here which are based on system interrupts should function on compatible hardware.

On the other hand, all these routines (of which there are not many) which directly address a memory zone or a port could cause problems. In this case, you will have to check through your system documentation to find out where the equivalent addresses are and make the corresponding modifications to the routines.

This is not the case for screen memory addressing as most manufacturers of compatible machines or boards have accepted the screen buffer address values (B800H and B000H).

The procedures and functions in question are:

—SetKbd and ResetKbd
—Switch_video_on and switch_video_off
—BorderColor.

3 STRUCTURE OF THIS BOOK

The first chapter will go rapidly through the concepts needed for a general understanding of the book as a whole.

Each of the following chapters is concerned with a particular field of interest and begins with a review of the essential information needed for an understanding of the routines discussed in that chapter.

The various subjects we shall consider are:

—screen management
—window management
—graphics management
—joystick management
—keyboard management
—floppy disk management
—printer management
—input/output procedures and functions
—miscellaneous procedures and functions
—advice and appendices.

In each chapter, for each procedure or function, the following information will be given (if appropriate):

—syntax
—function of the procedure
—pseudo-code
—an explanation of the mechanism used
—listing
—necessary predeclarations
—notes
—restrictions on use.

The reader should understand that in each chapter our aim is to present a body of coherent information providing a specific service. Each chapter should therefore be capable of standing alone. Certain of the procedures proposed may be used independently of the others. Under these conditions the reader will have to check carefully whether they contain calls to other procedures or functions which will have to be declared beforehand. Any predeclarations necessary will always be mentioned.

The best solution is to copy the routines from each chapter, in the order in which they are described, and without leaving out any of the declarations, into a file which it will later be possible to include in programs by means of the command {$I filename.ext}.

Readers should also bear in mind that the order of the chapters is important, as certain procedures in one chapter may be used in later chapters. It is therefore a good idea to start by reading the book straight through in order to have a clearer idea of the contents of each chapter. The reader will then be able to study particular chapters in greater depth.

4 CONSISTENCY OF PROCEDURES AND DECLARATIONS

The reader may sometimes be surprised by the way in which procedures, taken on their own, have been written. Our aim was, however, to build up a coherent set of procedures, for each of the groups studied.

The writing of each procedure or function proposed should therefore always be considered from the point of view of its position within the group and the role that it plays in it.

Furthermore, within each chapter, procedures will be considered in the order in which they have to be declared, in order to avoid any possible ambiguity.

5 PROCEDURES USED ONLY AS UTILITIES

In certain chapters (in particular the one concerning screen management) a small number of procedures may seem simplistic to experienced programmers.

They are discussed all the same because they can be used in other procedures or because they form a coherent set which is of some particular interest. No detailed description will be given of any of them.

6 KEYWORDS AND CONVENTIONS

The immediate values given in certain calculations or variable assignments will generally be expressed in hexadecimal (either using the standard convention, e.g. 21H, or the Turbo Pascal convention e.g. $21). Certain processes are easier to understand in hex than in decimal. After all, the hexadecimal system was created for precisely that reason.

Bit notation will use the standard convention on the PC, i.e.:

—bits are numbered from 0 to 7 within a byte and from 0 to 15 within a word
—bit 0 is the least significant bit (the rightmost bit).

7 ALGORITHMS

Readers may feel that certain algorithms have not been fully optimized. This will generally be in order to make them easier to read, and any sacrifices made in terms of compactness of code or speed of execution will always be based on a desire to make the message clearer. Readers can always rewrite particular lines in a procedure once they have understood the mechanism.

In the same way, it has sometimes been necessary to choose one of two ways of executing a particular task. In such cases, it is always the most orthodox method, as defined by DOS, which has been preferred.

What is an orthodox procedure? IBM only guarantees upward compatibility of software with successive versions of DOS if they use DOS services systematically without direct access to memory. We shall sometimes break this rule if no other solution seems possible.

CHAPTER 1

General technical data

1 INTERRUPTS

The flexibility in programming allowed by the IBM PC is based on the interrupt mechanism. Just what is that mechanism?

Any task carried out by a computer system is based on the use, by a central processing unit, of various resources, mostly peripherals or internal system components.

It would be tedious, difficult and futile for the user to write routines making use directly of these resources. In practice, two software layers handle this tiresome and repetitive work for us:

—the BIOS + IBMBIO.COM
—the DOS operating system.

The BIOS (Basic Input Output System) forms the kernel of all the input/output routines in the system. It carries out operations that may seem simple a priori but are complex in practice (e.g. writing a sector to a floppy disk: the drive motor has to be started, its speed has to be checked, the flow of information to write has to be monitored, etc.).

It is the BIOS which carries out all these basic functions and we shall see later how it can be used.

DOS also takes responsibility for a whole series of services, but at a higher level. In a sense, we could say that it adds surplus value to the BIOS services. How can we access those services? By means of interrupts.

The lowest addresses in memory contain what are called interrupt levels. They are numbered from 1 to 256 and each contains four bytes representing the address of a routine executing the service corresponding to that interrupt number.

A call to an interrupt of any number leads to the systems saving the activity currently under way, and branching direct to the address contained in the interrupt level, followed by execution of the service requested, a return to the instruction that was awaiting execution when the interrupt was issued and the continued execution of the program

Next question: how is an interrupt issued?

Before Turbo Pascal (and, to be fair, one or two other high level languages), we had to use the assembler. Once a programmer has decided to use a high level language, he has to be dragged kicking and screaming back to the assembler.

Turbo Pascal provides two procedures allowing direct access to interrupts:

—Intr (number, params)
—MsDos (params).

A detailed description of the syntax of these procedures is given in your Turbo Pascal manual, but be sure you have understood the following:

Intr calls the BIOS service named by the 'number' parameter and uses variable *params* (which has a clearly defined structure that must be respected) to pass to it the parameters necessary to execute the routine.

Params must be of the following type:
record
AX, BX, CX, DX, BP, SI, DI, DS, ES, FLAGS: integer; end;

The components of params represent the various registers of the Intel 8088 microprocessor in your PC. They will be loaded with the parameters which we pass to the interrupt routine and they return the results of the operation, if there are any.

Note that each of these registers is 16 bits long. In general, the values returned by the various services can be held in a byte. In such cases we will use the notation AH (the high AX byte), AL (the low AX byte), BH, BL, etc.

It also has to be understood that certain parameters will be passed to the interrupt routine by means of the high or low byte of the register in question alone. Sometimes there may even be one paramter in the high byte and another in the low byte. In such cases use will have to be made of bit offset or byte handling procedures such as Shl, Shr, Swap, etc. in order to load the parameter into the correct portion of the register. For data returned to a single byte of the register, we shall use the notation Hi (register) for the high byte and Lo (register) for the low byte.

MsDos calls a DOS service. The difference here between MsDos and Intr is minimal. When DOS is being used, the interrupt number is always 21H and what is in fact being requested is the execution of a subroutine which has a function number. This number is always loaded into the high byte of AX (this is also the case for passing function numbers to the BIOS). MsDos (params) is equivalent to Intr ($21, params).

Familiarity with interrupt numbers and the list of parameters to pass is obviously crucial if you want to make the most possible use of this facility. There is no need to worry if you do not have the necessary documentation, as the chapters that follow will study all the interrupts from which we can derive any benefit. That is one of the main aims of this book.

NB:

The register record type as described above will be declared systematically in all the procedures and functions using interrupts. This is intended to ease reading, but a little space can be saved by declaring the type once and for all and removing its declaration from the indicated procedures used.

2 MEMORY ADDRESSES

The space addressable by the INTEL 8088 in your PC is one megabyte. This is a lot, and in particular it is more than can be addressed directly by the 16 bit word which is the basic information unit of the microprocessor.

To make addressing possible, segmentation is used:

—we start by defining in which 64K *segment* the object to be addressed is held, and this segment address is held in one word (16 bits, the length of an integer in Turbo Pascal).

—we then specify the position (*offset*) of the object addressed with respect to the origin of the segment.

Combining these two values gives a logical address which can be written as follows:

segment: offset.

It is these values which will be returned by the standard functions Seg and Ofs which we shall be using considerably in what follows. It is also these values which will be used for direct reading and writing in memory using the predefined memory arrays Mem and MemW.

The use of the *debug* program which is provided with your DOS will show you how to handle these concepts. If you use this program to examine specific memory addresses you will see that the high order and low order bytes are inverted. This is a consequence of the way the 8088 works.

3 PORTS

Ports are specific locations, selected by a process different from that of memory address selection and acting as data transfer interfaces between the processor and its peripherals. We shall see that it can be useful to manipulate some of them but we shall always have to do so carefully, as some are for read only, others for write only and a third class for reading and writing.

They are selected by assigning values to the standard array Port for writing or reading a byte and so PortW for writing or reading a whole word.

CHAPTER 2

Screen handling

1 ESSENTIAL INFORMATION

1.1 Screen modes

The IBM PC allows various ways of displaying information: in 40 or 80 column wide text, or in medium or high resolution graphics. These are the various display modes. The BIOS uses the following numbers for them:

from 0 to 3: 25 row text modes

0: 40 columns, monochrome
1: 40 columns, colour
2: 80 columns, monochrome
3: 80 columns, colour

from 4 to 6: graphics modes

4: 320×200 colour
5: 320×200 monochrome
6: 640×200 colour
7: refers to the monochrome screen.

1.2 Screen memory

The information to display will be contained in part of the 8088's addressable memory space called the screen memory or screen buffer. It is here that circuits implementing display functions collect the necessary information.

The segment address of this buffer depends on the configuration of your system. With a monochrome screen, the address is B000H, while with a colour/graphics adaptor the address is B800H. This is of major importance if you want to write routines acceptable to both types of configuration.

1.3 Organization of screen memory

The way in which information is held in this memory varies according to the current screen mode (selected using standard Turbo Pascal procedures).

1.3.1 Text modes

For text modes, each character displayed takes up two bytes in the screen buffer: one byte for the character code and one byte for its display attribute (i.e. the way it is displayed, its colour, the background colour, whether it is blinking or not, etc.).

The structure of this byte is as follows:

—bits 0 to 2	:	character colour code
—bit 3	:	0 low intensity 1 high intensity
—bits 4 to 6	:	background colour code
—bit 7	:	0 normal character 1 blinking character.

The character codes are stored in bytes with even addresses and attributes are stored in bytes with odd addresses.

It is therefore easy to modify the display directly by changing the screen buffer. There is, however, a significant limitation to such activity: direct operations on the buffer lead to a 'snowstorm' effect, i.e. momentary parasite effects on the display, unless it is handled by a routine which would be difficult to write in anything but assembler. This in no way affects program execution (indeed many programs sold on the market use this method) but in the long term it becomes unpleasant and tiring to the eye. We shall therefore not use this method except in very special cases and for very brief operations.

The disadvantages above only occur with the graphic/colour adaptor in text mode.

1.3.2 Graphics modes

In graphics mode, pixels, i.e. elementary screen points, are addressed directly.

In medium resolution mode there are 320 × 200 pixels, making a total of 64 000 addressable points. With 16K of memory available we can therefore assign two bits to each point to define its colour. In high resolution, only one bit can be assigned to each pixel.

This is why only four colours can be defined in medium resolution and only two in high resolution.

In 320 × 200 mode, each byte represents 4 pixels.
In 640 × 200 mode, each byte represents 8 pixels.
(for further explanations, see the chapter on graphics.)

1.4 Screen pages

It is easy to deduce from what we have been saying that, in text mode, there is a great deal of space left available in the screen buffer. The 80 × 25 characters will occupy just a quarter of that memory.

It would be a pity to waste all that space. This concern led to the introduction of the concept of a screen page. A screen page is a 4K space in the screen buffer in 80 column mode or 2K in 40 column mode. That space can be displayed on request by certain BIOS services. It is even possible to write to one page while displaying another.

This facility is used by IBM BASIC. It is not the case in Turbo Pascal. We shall see how we can remedy this situation even though we cannot give a 100% solution to the problem.

1.5 Interrupts

It is interrupt 16 (10H) of the BIOS which implements all the routines concerning the screen display. Of the 16 existing services, nine are particularly interesting as they do not correspond to standard procedures in Turbo Pascal.

2 AIMS OF THIS CHAPTER

In this chapter we shall present a group of procedures whose main themes are as follows:

—cursor management
—screen page handling
—reading of characters from the screen
—assistance in screen creation
—display attribute handling
—various utility procedures.

The issues will not necessarily be examined in this particular order, since certain tools have to be developed before we can move on to those dealing with other issues.

3 PROCEDURES AND FUNCTIONS

3.1 Procedure GetVideo

In order to write procedures that can be used generally and independently of the current screen mode, it is absolutely necessary to have a tool allowing us to determine at any time what the current display situation is. This will be the role assigned to procedure GetScreen which we shall use frequently in this chapter and the next two.

syntax: GetScreen;

function:

Returns information about the current video mode, through the following global variables:

screen_mode	(byte):	number of the current mode
colnum	(byte):	number of text columns
page_disp	(byte):	page currently displayed.

pseudo-code:

a. load into AH function number 15
b. call interrupt 10H
c. return screen_mode in AL
   colnum in AH
   page_disp in BH.

mechanism:

Straightforward application of a BIOS call.

listing:

```
var
    screen_mode,colnum,page_disp:byte;

procedure GetScreen;

type
    result = record
               AX,BX,CX,DX,BP,SI,DI,DS,ES,flags:integer;
             end;
```

```
var
    params: result;

begin

params.AX:=$0F00;            {$0F: BIOS function number}

intr(16,params);

screen_mode:=Lo(params.AX);    {mode in AL}
colnum     :=Hi(params.AX);   {columns in AH}
page_disp  :=Hi(params.BX);   {page number in BH}

end;
```

predeclarations: None.

NOTES:

This procedure is fundamental and will be used in a great number of procedures we shall be examining later. Another way of carrying out this task is to write three functions (e.g. ScreenMode, ColNum and PageDisp) each of which uses the same interrupt. In this case, a good deal of the code would be duplicated. We felt it was preferable to create a single procedure and three global variables.

This is the approach we shall adopt throughout the book each time the number of parameters to obtain makes it worth it.

restrictions on use: None.

3.2 Cursor management procedures

It is indispensable, if we want to handle the screen display in an intelligent way, to have a series of simple cursor management procedures available allowing us to avoid continuous recourse to GoToXY type commands and the tedious calculations they make necessary. Management of the curser display is also important as it will make it possible to highlight parts of your programs. It will also be useful to be able to make it disappear at wish, producing a more attractive screen.

Procedure SetCursor;

syntax: SetCursor (init, final);

init and final are of integer type.

function:

Controls the shape of the cursor.

pseudo-code:

a. load into AH function number 1
b. load init into CH
c. load final into CL
d. call interrupt no 16.

mechanism:

Simple call to the BIOS.

The cursor is made up of superimposed lines numbered 0 to 7 (or 13 on the monochrome screen), starting from the top. You simply have to specify the starting line and the end line to give the cursor the required size.

The default values in the system are init = 6 and final = 7 (12 and 13 for the monochrome screen).

Note that it is impossible to control cursor blinking, which is a hardware function.

listing:

```
procedure SetCursor (init,final:integer);

type
    result = record
               AX,BX,CX,DX,BP,SI,DI,DS,ES,flags:integer;
             end;

var
    params:result;

begin
params.AX:=$100;                    {calls function 1}
params.CX:=init SHL 8 or final;     {init in CH}
                                    {final in CL}

intr(16,params);
end;
```

predeclarations: None.

NOTES:

Remember to give the cursor back its normal shape on exit from your program.

restrictions on use: None.

Procedure CsrOn

syntax: CsrOn;

function:

Returns the cursor to its normal state.

pseudo-code:

a. test the screen mode and defines the start and end lines
b. load into AH function number 1
c. load into CH 6 (or 12) and 7 (or 13) into CL
d. call interrupt 16.

mechanism:

As SetCursor.

listing:

```
procedure CsrOn;

type

     result = record
                AX,BX,CX,DX,BP,SI,DI,DS,ES,flags:integer;
              end;

var
params: result;
line_set:integer;

begin
GetScreen;
case screen_mode of            {defines the cursor according to
                                the screen type}
    0..3: line_set:=$0607;
    7   : line_set:=$0C0D;
end;

params.AX:=$100;              {calls function 1}
params.CX:=line_set;
intr(16,params);

end;
```

declarations: None.

NOTES: Simplified form of procedure SetCursor.

restrictions on use: None.

Procedure CsrOff

syntax: CsrOff;

function:

Turns the cursor off.

pseudo-code:

a. test the screen mode and define start and end lines
b. load function number 1 into AH
c. load value greater than 7 (or 13) into CH
d. load 7 (or 13) into CL
e. call screen interrupt 16.

mechanism:

Giving init a value greater than 7 (or 13) and final a value of 7 (or 13) disables the cursor display.

listing:

```
procedure CsrOff;

type
    result = record
               AX,BX,CX,DX,BP,SI,DI,DS,ES,flags:integer;
              end;

var
    params: result;
    line_set:integer;

begin

GetScreen;
case screen_mode of          {trick to disable the cursor}
    0..3: line_set:=$0807;
    7   : line_set:=$0E0D;
end;

params.AX:=$100;
params.CX:=line_set;

intr(16,params);

end;
```

declarations: None.

NOTES:

Enable the cursor before leaving the program.

restrictions on use: None.

Cursor Addressing Procedures

We shall not insult the reader's intelligence by giving detailed explanations of the following procedures. They do, however, provide an easier way of moving the cursor.

syntax:

GoNext;	Bottom;	EndLine;	ClrLineToCsr;
GoPred;	Top;	BeginLine;	ClrLine;

listings:

```
procedure GoNext;    {in a window, use GoNextWin}
```

```
{moves the cursor to the next logical position}
{if the cursor is at position colnum,25...}
{return to 1,1}

begin

if WhereX <> colnum
    then
        GoToXY(WhereX+1,WhereY)
    else
        if WhereY = 25
        then GoToXY(1,1)          {return if at end of screen}
        else GoToXY(1,WhereY+1);

end;

procedure GoPred;    {in a window use GoPredWin}

{moves the cursor to the preceding logical position}
{if the cursor is at position 1,1...}
{... return to colnum, 25}

begin
if WhereX <> 1
    then
    GoToXY(WhereX-1,WhereY)
    else
    if WhereY = 1         {return if at top of screen}
        then GoToXY(colnum,25)
        else GoToXY(colnum,WhereY-1);
end;

procedure Top;

{take the cursor back to the top of the screen leaving X
unchanged}

begin
    GoToXY(WhereX,1);
end;

procedure Bottom;

{as before but to the bottom of screen}

begin
    GoToXY(WhereX,25);
end;
```

```
procedure BeginLine;

{move the cursor to the start of a line}

begin
    GoToXY(1,WhereY);
end;

procedure EndLine;  {do not use within a window}

{move cursor to the end of a line}

begin
    GetScreen;
    GoToXY(colnum,WhereY);
end;

procedure Jump(n:integer);     {n may be negative}

{jump n lines}

begin
    if (WhereY+n) in [1..25]
    then
        GoToXY(WhereX,WhereY+n)
    else
        if WhereY+n<1 then GoToXY(WhereX,1)    {at top of
screen}
                     else GoToXY(WhereX,25); {at bottom of
screen}
end;

procedure ClrLine;

{delete the current line}

begin
    CsrOff;
    BeginLine;
    ClrEol;
    CsrOn;
end;

procedure ClrLineToCsr;

{delete the line up to the cursor position}

var keepx:byte;
```

```
begin
     CsrOff;
     keepx:=Wherex;
     BeginLine;
     repeat write (' '); until WhereX=keepx;
     CsrOn;
end;
```

declarations: Procedures GetScreen, CsrOn, CsrOff.

NOTES:

GoNext and GoPred do not apply to windows where GoNextWin and GoPredWin are used instead. On condition that all the screen and window procedures are declared it is, however, easy to write a common procedure using a boolean variable which is read during selection, and which shows whether we are in full screen mode or not. In the latter case, the system knows what screen limits to use (see the window management procedures).

restrictions on use:

GoNext and Gopred are relatively slow procedures. For scans across large areas, it is better to use traditional iterative structures.

Procedure SetTab

syntax: SetTab (t);

t is of the byte type.

function:

Create a cursor tab position.

pseudo-code:

a. test the screen mode
b. if t is a valid tab position...
c. include t in the set of tab positions
d. else, do nothing.

mechanism:

Illustrates the extremely useful nature of sets. Imagine trying to write the same routine without this facility...

listing:

```
type tabset = set of 1..80;

const RefTabSet: tabset = [];

{defines all the tab positions}
{as being empty}
```

```
procedure SetTab(t:byte);

begin
    GetScreen;
    if t in [1..colnum] then RefTabSet:=RefTabSet +[t];
    {include the new position}
end;
```

declarations: Procedure GetScreen.

restrictions on use:

Will have to be modified to be used in window mode.

Procedure ClearTab

syntax: ClearTab (t);

t is of byte type.

function:

Clears a tab position.

pseudo-code:

a. if the tab position exists.
b. if clear...

mechanism:

As above.

listing:

```
procedure ClearTab(t:byte);

begin
    if t in RefTabSet then RefTabSet:=RefTabSet-[t];
    {removes an element from the set}
end;
```

declarations: Procedure GetScreen.

NOTES: As for SetTab.

restrictions on use: None.

Procedure GoNextTab

syntax: GoNextTab;

function:

Send the cursor to the next tab position starting from the current position.

pseudo-code:

a. test the screen mode
b. go to the next logical cursor position...
c. until it is equal to a tab position or the end of the line has been reached.

mechanism:

Use of a set structure for tab positions avoids the need to write complicated code.

listing:

```
procedure GoNextTab;

begin
    GetVideo;
    repeat
    GoNext;
    until (WhereX in RefTabSet) or (WhereX=colnum);
end;
```

declarations: Procedures GetScreen, SetTab, ClearTab.

NOTES: None.

restrictions on use: As above.

3.3 Procedure ScreenDump

It is sometimes useful in the course of a program to be able to dump a screen as it appears to the user without requiring him to touch any keys. ScreenDump prints the screen contents using code for which the least that can be said is that it is very concise...

syntax: ScreenDump;

function:

Prints the screen contents.

pseudo-code:

a. save register BP
b. call interrupt number five
c. restore register BP.

mechanism:

Interrupt five produces a full dump of the screen currently being displayed. Here the call is made directly since no parameter is passed or returned. We therefore use instruction inline to introduce machine code directly:

$55	means PUSH BP
$CD/$05	means INT 5
$5D	means POP BP

listing:

```
procedure ScreenDump;

begin

inline($55/$CD/$05/$5D);{direct call to interrupt number 5}
end;
```

declarations: None.

NOTES:

If the screen to dump is a graphics screen, it is essential to execute the DOS command GRAPHICS before executing the program.

Function PrinterOk, which we shall consider in the chapter on printing, can be used to check that the printer is available.

3.4 Procedures Switch_screen_off and Switch_screen_on

We shall see later that it is sometimes necessary, in the course of certain screen memory handling processes, to disable the screen temporarily to avoid certain parasitic visual effects. This is the role of these two procedures.

syntax: Switch_screen_off and
Switch_screen_on;

function:

Disables or enables the screen but without loss of any of the screen contents.

pseudo-code:

a. test the display mode
b. set bit 3 of port 3D8H to 0 or 1 while leaving the values of the other bits unchanged.

mechanism:

Port 3D8H of the colour/graphic adaptor manages the screen mode. Bit 3 defines whether or not display is to take place. Handling it is made more complicated by the fact that it is a write only port. We therefore have to reconstitute the whole byte for each mode concerned, using the following information:

bit 0	0 = 40 column mode	1 = 80 column mode
bit 1	0 = text mode	1 = graphics mode
bit 2	0 = colour	1 = monochrome
bit 3	0 = no display	1 = normal
bit 4	0 = 320 × 200	1 = 640 × 200

bit 5 allows a choice between:

0 = up to 16 background colours but no blinking
1 = characters may blink but only eight background colours are available.

listing:

```
procedure Switch_Screen_off;

begin
     GetScreen;
     case screen_mode of
     0:   Port [$3D8]:=$24;     {set bit 3 at port $3D8}
     1:   Port [$3D8]:=$20;     {no and possible:}
     2:   Port [$3D8]:=$25;     {port write-only}
     3:   Port [$3D8]:=$21;
     end;
end;

procedure switch_display_on;

begin
     GetScreen;
     case screen_mode of
     0:   Port [$3D8]:=$2C;    {set the same bit to 1}
     1:   Port [$3D8]:=$28;    {digit 2 may be changed}
     2:   Port [$3D8]:=$2D;    {to 0 : 16 background colours}
     3:   Port [$3D8]:=$29;    {are then allowed}
     end;
end;
```

declarations: GetScreen.

NOTES:

The value of these procedures is that they inhibit display during direct manipulation of the screen memory, so as to hide the parasytic effects produced (snowstorm effect).

This therefore only applies to text mode. Other uses may well be possible. It has no effect on a monochrome screen.

The fact that the screen has been switched off does not prevent a display being built up. This means that we can make a screen appear instantaneously by inhibiting display while it is being written.

As we specified, the fact that bit 5 is set to 0 provides the possibility of producing 16 background colours instead of 8. This does not, however, mean that the standard procedure text background will be able to draw on all 16. To do so, we shall have to use the extended display procedures discussed below and check the background character by character.

restrictions on use:

Be careful when handling this port.

3.5 Procedure CopyPage

It would be a great pity to waste all the screen memory that is left unused by the standard Turbo Pascal write procedures. Without rivalling the sophisticated use made of that space by IBM BASIC, we can still take advantage of some of it using the CopyPage procedure, which allows us to hold three text screens in 80 column mode and 7 in 40 column mode, and display them later instantaneously by means of the DispPage procedure.

syntax: CopyPage (n1, n2);

n1 and n2 are of the byte type.

function:

Saves screen page n1 in screen page n2 in order to use it later by means of DispPage (n).

Page n1 is unmodified.

pseudo-code

a. test the screen mode
b. if it is a text mode...
c. disable the display
d. transfer the contents of page n1 into page n2
e. enable the display.

mechanism:

The trick here is to define two screen page arrays:

—one 8 × 2k array for the 40 column mode
—one 4 × 4k array for the 80 column mode

The arrays are defined in absolute addresses with their point of origin at the start of the screen memory.

All that remains to be done is to assign the value of element n1 of the array to element n2.

Remember, however, that Turbo Pascal can only write to page 0.

listing:

```
procedure CopyPage(n1,n2:byte);

type

ScreenBuffer40 = array[0..7,1..2048] of byte; {8 40-column
pages}
ScreenBuffer80 = array[0..3,1..4096] of byte; {4 80-column
pages}

var

display40:ScreenBuffer40 absolute $B800:0;{position the
variables}
display80:ScreenBuffer80 absolute $B800:0;{in the screen
buffer}
```

```
begin

GetScreen;
if screen_mode in [0..3] then

case colnum of

40:   begin
         switch_screen_off;
         display40[n2]:=display40[n1]; {page n2 = page n1}
         switch_display_on;
      end;

80:   begin
         switch_screen_off;
         display80[n2]:=display80[n1];
         switch_display_on;
      end;
end;

end;
```

declarations: Procedure GetScreen, Switch_screen_off, Switch_display_on.

NOTES:

Causes the screen to flicker briefly during transfer of the screen variable.

This procedure is useful if you need to store screens which have to be displayed rapidly, e.g. help screens, which can be saved in buffer memory (e.g. perhaps at the beginning of the program). Note too that ClrScr affects the page being displayed.

THIS PROCEDURE IS INDEPENDENT OF THE TEXT MODE BEING USED.

If the current mode is 80 columns there are 3 buffer pages + 1 normal display page and if the current mode is 40 columns, there are 7 buffer pages + 1 normal page.

This procedure has no effect on the monochrome screen.

restrictions on use:

Text modes only, with the graphics/colour adaptor.

3.6 Procedure DispPage

DispPage is the procedure allowing instantaneous display of screen pages saved using CopyPage or written directly using the extended display procedures.

syntax: DispPage (n);

n is of the byte type.

function:

Leads to instantaneous display of page n which was previously stored using CopyPage, WriteAt or WriteAttribute.

pseudo-code:

a. test display mode
b. if it is a text mode...
c. load function number 5 into AH and the number of the page to display into AL
d. call display interrupt 16.

mechanism:

Simple call to the BIOS.

listing:

```
procedure DispPage(n:byte);

type
    result = record
               AX,BX,CX,DX,BP,SI,DI,DS,ES,flags:integer;
             end;

var
    params: result;

begin
    GetScreen;
    if screen_mode in [0..3] then  {no effect on monochrome
                                     screen}
    begin
    params.AX:=$500 or n;       {function no 5 - call page n}
    intr(16,params);
    end;
end;
```

declarations: Procedure GetScreen.

NOTES:

It is up to the user to see to page management and to ensure that calls are consistent with the current display mode.

Turbo Pascal does not allow writing to pages other than page 0. The screens to save must therefore always be written in page 0 before being transferred.

The following procedures, on the other hand, do allow data to be written to any page, but only by making certain concessions which the user will undoubtedly understand.

restrictions on use:

Text mode only.
No effect on the monochrome screen.

3.7 Procedure Locate

In order to write directly to a screen page which is not page 0 (an operation that is not allowed in standard Turbo Pascal), we first have to be able to send the cursor to it in an appropriate way:

syntax: Locate (n, column, row);

n, column and row are all of integer type.

function:

Positions the cursor in page n at the location specified. That location will be used by procedures WriteAt and WriteAttribute to write one or more identical characters.

pseudo-code:

a. test the display mode
b. if it is a text mode...
c. load function number 2 into AH
d. load the page number
e. load the row and column numbers, in the form required by BIOS conventions, into DH and DL
f. call the display interrupt.

mechanism:

Simple call to the BIOS.

listing:

```
procedure Locate (n,column,row:integer)

type
    result = record
               AX,BX,CX,DX,BP,SI,DI,DS,ES,flags:integer;
             end;

var
    params:result;

begin
GetScreen;
if screen_mode in [0..3] then
    begin
    params.AX:=$200;                  {function no 2}
    params.BX:=n SHL 8;               {pass the page number}
    column:=column-1;row:= row-1;     {BIOS reference : 0 rather
                                       than 1}
    params.DX:=row SHL 8 or column;   {pass row and column
                                        number}

    intr(16,params);
```

```
    end;

end;
```

declarations: Procedure GetScreen.

NOTES:

A cursor position can be determined for each page.
No effect on the monochrome screen.

restrictions on use: Text mode only.

3.8 Procedure WriteAt

Now that we have sent the cursor to the page and position we want, we just have to start writing. To do so there are just two BIOS functions available to us, both of them relatively limited but both capable of providing immense assistance, as we shall see in our chapter on window management. The first of these BIOS functions is WriteAt which we shall consider here, the second is WriteAttribute which we shall consider after procedure ReadScreen.

syntax: WriteAt (ch, n, m);

ch is of character type, n and m are of integer type.

function:

Writes character ch, m times over, in page n, at the current position of the cursor for that page.

pseudo-code:

a. test the display mode
b. if it is a text mode…
c. load function number n into AH
d. load the character code into AL
e. load the page number into BH
f. load the number of characters to write into CL
g. call the display interrupt.

mechanism:

Simple call to the BIOS.

listing:

```
procedure WriteAt(ch:char;n,m:integer);

type
    result = record
               AX,BX,CX,DX,BP,SI,DI,DS,ES,flags:integer;
             end;
```

```
var
    params:result;

begin

GetScreen;
if screen_mode in [0..3] then

begin
params.AX:=$A00 or ord(ch);      {function $A, pass character}
params.BX:=n SHL8;               {pass page number}
params.CX:=m;                    {pass number of characters}
intr(16,params);
end;
end;
```

declarations: Procedure GetVideo.

NOTES:

Attributes cannot be specified using this procedure.
No effect on monochrome screens.
This basic procedure can be used to build up routines to display character strings in any screen page.

restrictions on use:

Text mode only.

3.9 Procedure ReadScreen

BASIC allows characters to be read from the screen, which Turbo Pascal does not. However, with a little effort we can add this facility, which will be immensely useful to us later.

syntax: ReadScreen;

function:

Returns the character and attribute at the current position of the cursor, in the global variables scrn_char and attr;

scrn_char is of character type,
attr is of byte type.

pseudo-code:

a. load function number 8 into AH
b. load page number into BH
c. call display interrupt
d. obtain the character code read from AL...
e. ...and its attribute in AH.

mechanism:

Simple BIOS call.

listing:

```
var scrn_char:char; {global variables referenced by other
                     procedures}
        attr:byte; {character read and its attribute}

procedure ReadScreen;

type
    result = record
              AX,BX,CX,DX,BP,SI,DI,DS,ES,flags:integer;
             end;

var
    params:result;

begin
    params.AX:=$800;     {function 8}
    params.BX:=0;        {page 0}

    intr(16,params);

    scrn_char:=chr(Lo(params.AX));      {character read from
                                         AL}
        attr:=Hi(params.AX);            {attribute in AH}
end;
```

declarations: None.

NOTES:

This procedure can be extremely useful: we shall use it in a number of procedures for screen management and for text window management.

It can also be used in graphics mode. In this case, no attribute is read.

If a page other than page 0 is to be read, the page number will have to be passed through BH.

Note too that it is possible to read the position of the cursor in the chosen page. The function number 3 has to be used and the page number is passed through BH.

The current row will be in DH and the column in DL. But be careful: the origin, at the top left, is 0,0 and not 1,1. We did not feel it was useful to implement this procedure, but, if you need it, you can easily build it up using the ideas above. It is simply necessary to establish an extended version of WhereX and WhereY, which are standard functions.

restrictions on use: None.

3.10 Function Attribute

Before we move on to a study of procedure WriteAttribute, we shall create a little utility allowing us to build up a screen attribute byte using the desired parameters, expressed explicitly.

syntax: Attribute (background, foreground);

background and foreground are of the byte type,
the value returned is of byte type.

function:

Returns a character display attribute byte, built up from the parameters passed, for use by procedure WriteAttribute.

Background = background colour
if >7, character is blinking.

Foreground = foreground colour
if >15, the character is blinking (base colour + 16).

(The predefined constants, blue, red, etc. may be used.)

E.g.: Attribute (lightblue, yellow) produces a blinking display attribute, at high intensity with a blue background and a green character.

pseudo-code:

a. set bit 7 to 1 if foreground >15
b. load the background colour into the high order half-byte
c. load the character colour into the low order half-byte.

mechanism:

See pseudo-code and comments on the attribute.

listing:

```
function Attribute(background,foreground:integer):byte;

var
    buffer : byte;

begin
if foreground>=16 then buffer:=$80 else buffer:=0;
                {blinking?}

buffer:=(buffer or (background shl 4)) or (foreground mod
                                                    16);
        {positions background and foreground colours}

Attribute:=buffer;
end;
```

declarations: None.

NOTES:

On the monochrome screen, if foreground = 1 and background = 0, the character is underlined.

The standard constants blue, yellow, red, etc... in Turbo Pascal are of course available.

restrictions on use: None.

3.11 Procedure WriteAttribute

This is a second procedure which allows us to write to the screen page of our choice at the cursor location. Above all, it is an indispensable supplement to procedure ReadScreen. With these two procedures, we can already see the possibility beginning to appear of reading a character and its attribute from the screen, to process the attribute in whatever way we like and to send the character and attribute back to the screen. This will be used in procedures to assist in screen creation and window handling.

syntax: WriteAttribute(n, ch, attribute);

n is of the integer type,
ch is of the character type,
attribute is of the byte type.

function:

Writes character ch with its attribute to the current position of the cursor in page n.

pseudo-code:

a. load function number 9 into AH
b. load the character code into AL
c. load the character attribute into BL
d. load the number of characters to write into CX
e. call the screen interrupt.

mechanism:

Simple BIOS call.

listing:

```
procedure
WriteAttribute(n:integer;character:char;attribute:byte);

type
    result = record
               AX,BX,CX,DX,BP,SI,DI,DS,ES,flags:integer;
              end;

var
    params:result;
```

```
begin
params.AX:=$0900 or ord(character); {function 9, pass
                                     character}
params.BX:=(n SHL 8) or attribute;  {pass page and attribute}
params.CX:=1;                       {only 1 character}

intr (16,params);
end;
```

declarations: None.

NOTES:

Apart from its use for the rest of this chapter and for window management, this procedure can be used in the same way as WriteAt but with the additional possibility of allowing us to write one or several characters with their attributes to the screen page of our choice.

The page number has no significance in graphics mode but has to be specified.

restrictions on use: None.

3.12 Procedure Scroll

Even though Turbo Pascal provide procedures DelLine and Insline, which can handle screen scrolling, it can be useful to have a specific procedure for this task, with the additional facility of allowing a choice of screen attribute for the spaces with which the screen fills up as it scrolls.

syntax: Scroll (direction, linecount, attribute, x1, y1, x2, y2);

direction is of boolean type,
all the other parameters are of integer type.

function:

Causes scrolling upwards or downwards by a number of lines equal to linecount, replacing the empty lines created by blank characters with the attribute 'attribute'.

If linecount = 0, the whole of the specified area is cleared.

The effect of the procedure is limited to the window specified by x1, y1 (top left-hand corner) and x2, y2 (bottom right-hand corner).

Scanning takes place upwards if direction is true and downwards otherwise.

pseudo-code:

a. load service number 6 or 7 into AH depending on the direction
b. load number of lines into AL
c. load the attribute into BX
d. load the coordinates of the top left-hand corner into CX
e. load the coordinate of the bottom right-hand corner into DX
f. call the display interrupt.

mechanism:

Simple BIOS call.
Why does 1 have to be subtracted from all coordinates?
Because BIOS references are not 1, colnum, 1, 25, but 0, colnum-1, 0, 24.

listing:

```
procedure Scroll(direction:boolean;linecount, attribute,
x1,y1,x2,y2:integer);

type
    result = record
              AX,BX,CX,DX,BP,SI,.DI,ES,flags:integer;
             end;

var
    params: result;
    function: integer;

begin
    if direction then function: = $600 else function:=$700;

params.AX:=function or linecount;  {function—number of
                                    lines}
params.BX:=attribute shl 8;        {attribute in BH}
params.CX:=(y1-1) shl 8 or (x1-1); {top left-hand corner in
                                    CX}
params.DX:=(y2-1) shl 8 or (x2-1); {bottom right-hand corner
                                    in DX}

intr(16,params);
end;
```

declarations: None.

NOTES:

Procedure Scroll can be used to produce certain particular effects, notably by taking advantage of the possibility of changing background by acting on the attribute parameter.

An adaptation of this procedure for windows is given in the following chapter.

restrictions on use: Text mode only.

3.13 Some small utilities to assist in plotting on screen

Displaying tables and menus is always a tedious exercise which needs to be made as easy as possible. The following procedures will help.

Procedure Box

syntax: Box (x1, y1, x2, y2, colour, line);

all these paramters are of the byte type.

function:

Draws a character frame with coordinates x1, y1 (top left-hand corner) and x2, y2 (bottom right-hand corner) in colour color and using single or double lines depending on whether the value of the line is one or two.

pseudo-code:

a. draw the top left-hand corner
b. draw the upper side and the top right-hand corner
c. draw the two vertical sides simultaneously
d. draw the bottom left-hand corner and the lower side
e. if the bottom right-hand corner is not the bottom of the screen...
f. draw the bottom right-hand corner
g. else...
h. test the display mode
i. deduce the position in screen memory of the bottom right-hand corner
j. write it directly to memory with the attribute of the character preceding it.

mechanism:

The only point worth examining in detail is the calculation of the position of the bottom right-hand corner in memory. If the latter character were written using procedure write, then if the frame filled the whole screen, it would scroll upwards, which would delete the upper side.

Writing the character directly to memory produces no cursor movement and therefore leaves the frame intact.

listing:

```
const LineChar:      array[1..2,1..15] of char =
((#218,#191,#192,#217,#196,#179,#195,#180,#194,#193,#197,#199,
#182,#209,#207),
(#201,#187,#200,#188,#205,#186,#204,#185,#203,#202,#206,#198,
#181,#210,#208));

procedure Box(x1,y1,x2,y2,color,line:byte);

var
    i,base,offset:integer;

begin

CsrOff;
TextColor(color);
gotoXY(x1,y1);write(LineChar[line,1]); {top left-hand corner}
```

```
for i:=x1+1 to x2-1 do write(LineChar[line,5]);{upper edge}
write(LineChar[line,2]);                        {top right-hand
                                                 corner}

for i:=y1+1 to y2-1 do                          {sides}
    begin
    gotoXY(x1,i);write(LineChar[line,6]);
    gotoXY(x2,i);write(LineChar[line,6]);
    end;

gotoXY(x1,y2);write(LineChar[line,3]);  {bottom left-hand
                                         corner}

for i:=x1+1 to x2-1 do write(LineChar[line,5]);  {lower edge}

if not((wherey=25) and (wherex=colnum)) {if not last}
then                                    {screen position...}
  write(LineChar[line,4])               {bottom right-hand
                                         corner}
else
begin
GetScreen;                               {else write to}
if screen_mode=7   then base:=$B000      {memory}
                    else base:=$B800;

if colnum=80        then offset:=$F9E   {4000th byte}
                    else offset:=$7CE;  {2000th byte}

Memw[base:offset]:=ord(LineChar[line,4]);
Memw[base:offset+1]:=Memw[base:offset-1]; {same attribute as}
                                         {preceding character}

end;
CsrOn;
end;
```

declarations: Procedure GetScreen.

NOTES:

An adapted form of this procedure will be presented in the chapter dealing with windows.

restrictions on use: Text mode only.

Procedures HLine, Vline, CxLine

syntax:

Hline (y,x1,x2,color,line);
Vline (x,y1,y2,color,line);
CXline (y,xh1,xh2,x,yv1,yv2,color,line);

all parameters are of the byte type.

function:

HLine:
Draws a horizontal line joining a box, at height y and between coordinates x1 and x2, in colour color and using a single or double line depending on whether the value of the line is one or two.

VLine:
The same for a vertical line.

CxLine:
Combination of HLine and VLine.
(Crossing lines with a cross at the intersection.)

listing:

```
procedure Hline(y,x1,x2,color,line:integer);

{line ends overlap at the vertical edges of the box}

var
    i: integer;

begin
    TextColor(color);
    gotoXY(x1,y);write(LineChar[line,7]);
    for i:=x1+1 to x2-1 do write (LineChar[line,5]);
    write(LineChar[line,8]);
end;

procedure Vline(x,y1,y2,color,line:integer);

{line ends overlap with the horizontal edges of the box}

var
    i: integer;

begin
    TextColor(color);
    gotoXY(x,y1);write(LineChar[line,9]);
    for i=y1+1 to y2-1 do
        begin
        gotoXY(x,i);
        write(LineChar[line,6]);
        end;
    gotoXY(x,y2);write(LineChar[line,10]);
    end;
```

```
procedure CXline (y,xh1,xh2,x,yv1,yv2,color,line:integer);

{HLine then VLine + cross at intersection}

begin
Hline(y,xh1,xh2,color,line);
Vline(x,yv1,yv2,color,line);
GotoXY(x,y);write(LineChar[line,11]);
end;
```

declarations: None.

restrictions on use: None.

3.14 Procedure FindScreenString

It may be of value in certain applications to have a way of simply finding a character string displayed on the screen without having to calculate coordinates. However, and this is a point we shall have to make again below, the fact that the procedure does not operate directly on memory makes it fairly slow. Do not use it unless there is a good chance of finding the string in question in an area fairly close to the current position of the cursor.

syntax: FindScreenString (str);

str is of the screenstring type or string [80].

function:

Finds the first occurrence of string str starting from the current position of the cursor.

Positions the cursor immediately after the string if the search succeeds and if after is true, otherwise leaves the cursor on the first character.

If the search fails, the cursor is positioned in the bottom right-hand corner of the screen.

pseudo-code:

a. for each position of the cursor from the current position...
b read the character displayed on the screen
c. compare it with the first character in the string
d. if equal...
   d1. read the next characters for a length equal to that of the string
   d2. if these strings are equal leave the loop
   d3. else return to the first character and continue the search
e. else continue the search until the final possible position is reached.

mechanism:

Use is made of procedure ReadScreen to read characters from the screen and of procedure GoNext to go from one logical cursor position to the next.

The display mode is tested to find out the number of columns and the cursor is switched off until the end of the search procedure is reached.

listing:

```
type ScreenString = string[80];

var  StringFound:  boolean;

procedure FindScreenString(str:screenstring;after:boolean);

procedure SearchString;  {search sub-procedure}

var
    pos,keepx,keepy,i  : integer;
              buffer   : screenstring;

begin
pos:=(WhereX-1)+((WhereY-1)*colnum);     {find current
                                          position}
                                         {in screen buffer}
repeat
ReadScreen;            {reads the character at the current
                        position}
if scrn_char=str[1] then {if equal to first character of the
                          string...}
begin
buffer:='';                                   {read the rest}
keepx:=WhereX;keepy:=WhereY;
for i:=1 to Length(str) do    begin
                              buffer:=buffer + scrn_char;
                              GoNext;
                              ReadScreen;
                              end;
GoToXY(keepx,keepy);              {return to starting point}
StringFound:=(buffer=str);        {strings equal?}
end;
pos:=Succ(pos);
GoToXY((pos mod colnum)+1,pos div colnum +1); {move forward
                                                a position}
until StringFound or ((WhereX=colnum) and (WhereY=25));

if StringFound then              {position the cursor}
begin
    GoPred;
    if after then for i:=1 to Length (str) do GoNext;
    end;

end;

begin                            {body of the routine}
    CsrOff;
    GetScreen;
```

```
    StringFound:=false;
    SearchString;
    CsrOn;
end;
```

declarations: GetScreen, CsrOn, CsrOff, ReadScreen, GoNext, GoPred.

NOTES:

The string may stretch over two lines but it may not be more than 80 characters long.

This procedure is useful in screen handling but has the disadvantage of being rather slow. The low search speed is due to the fact that instead of working on a memory buffer, as in text handling, it makes use of the ReadScreen procedure. This avoids the usual disadvantages of direct read or write operations to the screen memory (snowstorm effect).

The boolean variable StringFound is updated to allow the use of procedure ReplaceScreenString or for other such uses.

restrictions on use: Text mode only.

3.15 Procedure ReplaceScreenString

This is the logical sequel to the previous procedure.

syntax: ReplaceScreenString (str1, str2, after);

str1 and str2 are of the screenstring or string [80] type.

function:

Starting from the present cursor position, find string str1 on the screen and replace it with string str2. If after is true the cursor is positioned at the end of the string, otherwise it remains on the first character of the word.

pseudo-code:

a. check that the two strings are of the same length
b. if so, starting from the present cursor position, find the first on the screen
c. if found: replace.

mechanism:

Uses procedure FindScreenString.

listing:

```
procedure ReplaceScreenString (str1,str2:screenstring;after:
boolean);

var
    jump: integer;

begin
if Length(str1)=Length(str2) then {this check not obligatory}
```

```
begin
FindScreenString(str1,false);        {find the string}
if StringFound then
then
write(str2);                         {if found, replace}
if not after then    {if after is false return to start of
                      the word}
begin
if WhereX-Length(str1)<=0 then jump:=1 else jump:=0;
GotoXY((colnum*jump)+WhereX-Length(str1),WhereY-jump);
end;
end;
end;
end;
```

declarations: Procedures GetScreen, ReadScreen, CsrOn, CsrOff, FindScreenString, GoNext, GoPred.

NOTES:

The last two procedures along with colour and attribute manipulation procedures will allow the use of special effects to enhance menus and other screens. (See below.)

The requirement that the strings should be of equal length is there only for security reasons and can be dropped.

restrictions on use: Text mode only.

3.16 Procedure BorderColor

Some people may want to be able to select the colour of the screen frame in text mode. This simple procedure allows them to do so easily.

syntax: BorderColor (color);

color is of byte type.

function:

Defines the colour of the screen frame in text mode.

pseudo-code:

a. test the display mode
b. if the mode is 1 or 3...
c. load the colour into port 3D9H.

mechanism:

Among other specific roles already used by Turbo Pascal, port 3D9H defines the colour of the frame in text colour mode.

It is also by using this port that Turbo Pascal obtains two additional palettes in medium resolution graphics mode.

listing:

```
procedure BorderColor(color:integer);

begin
    GetScreen;
    if screen_mode in [1,3] then Port [$3D9]:=color mod16;
end;
```

declarations: Procedure GetScreen.

restrictions on use: Text mode only.

3.17 Function GetBackground

To make screen attribute handling easier we may need this simple function returning the colour of the background.

syntax: GetBackground;

the value returned is of the byte type.

function:

Returns the colour of the background at the cursor location.

pseudo-code:

a. read the screen character attribute
b. read bits 4 to 6 and returns them.

mechanism:

Use of ReadScreen.

listing:

```
function GetBackGround:byte;

begin
    ReadScreen;
    GetBackGround:=(attr and $70) shr 4; {reads bits 4..6 of
                                          the attribute}
end;
```

declarations: Procedure ReadScreen.

NOTES:

A useful function for the use of procedure Invert. (See 3.21.)

restrictions on use: Text mode only.

3.18 Procedures Hilite and LoLite

These procedures and those following allow highlighting of parts of the screen without repeated use of TextColor and TextBackGround. They form a complete set which is very flexible to use. They are all based on attribute transformations.

Note that these procedures, like ReadScreen, WriteAt and WriteAttribute, do not cause the cursor to move.

syntax: Hilite;
LoLite;

function:

The character at the current cursor position is displayed at high or low intensity respectively.

pseudo-code:

a. read the character and its attribute
b. set bit 3 of the attribute to 1 or 0
c. rewrite the character and its attribute.

mechanism:

Use of ReadScreen and WriteAttribute.

listing:

```
procedure Hilite;

begin
ReadScreen;
attr:=attr or $08;          {sets bit 3 of attribute 1 to 1}
WriteAttribute(0,scrn_char,attr);  {returns the attribute to
                                     the screen}
end;

procedure LoLite;

begin
ReadScreen;
attr:=attr and $F7;                {sets the same bit to 0}
WriteAttribute(0,scrn_char,attr);
end;
```

declarations: Procedures ReadScreen, WriteAttribute.

restrictions on use: Text mode only.

3.19 Procedures CharBlink and NoBlink

syntax: CharBlink;
NoBlink;

function:

The character at the current cursor position starts to blink or stops blinking.

pseudo-code:

a. read the character and its attribute
b. set bit 7 of the attribute to 1 or 0
c. rewrite the character and its attribute.

mechanism:

As for Hilite.

listing:

```
procedure CharBlink;

begin
ReadScreen;
attr:=attr or $80;        {sets bit 7 of the attribute to 1}
WriteAttribute(0,scrn_char,attr);
end;

procedure NoBlink;

begin
ReadScreen;
attr:=attr and $7F;       {set same bit to 0}
WriteAttribute(0,scrn_char,attr);
end;
```

declarations: Procedures ReadScreen, WriteAttribute.

restrictions on use: Text mode only.

3.20 Procedure CharColor

syntax: CharColor (color);

color is of the byte type.

function:

Gives the character at the current cursor position the colour color.
If color is >15, the character will blink.

pseudo-code:

a. read the character and its attribute
b. modify bits 0 and 3 and possibly bit 7 (blinking)
c. display the character and its new attribute.

mechanism:

See pseudo-code.

listing:

```
procedure CharColor(color:byte);
```

```
begin

ReadScreen;
if color > 15 then attr:=attr or $80;   {blinking if required}
attr:=(attr and $F8) or (color and $0F);{mask the background}
WriteAttribute(0,scrn_char,attr);
end;
```

declarations: Procedures ReadScreen, WriteAttribute.

restrictions on use: None.

3.21 Procedure Invert

syntax: Invert (color);

color is of the byte type.

function:

Gives the background of the current cursor position the colour of the character, and sets the character colour to color.

pseudo-code:

a. read the character and attribute
b. mask the attribute to conserve the blinking and high intensity bits
c. load bits 4 to 6 with bits 0 to 2 and load bits 0 to 2 with color
d. rewrite the character and its attribute.

mechanism:

Transferring bits within the attribute may seem a little obscure, but analysing the procedure carefully will show how it works.

listing:

```
procedure  Invert(color:byte);

const buffer: byte = $88;      {mask to conserve bits 3 and 7}

begin
ReadScreen;
buffer:=buffer and attr;
attr:=(buffer or ((attr and $07) shl 400 or (color and $0F);
if color > 16 then attr:=attr or $80;     {exchanges colours}
                                         {blinks if required}

WriteAttribute (0,scrn_char,attr);
end;
```

declarations: Procedures ReadScreen, WriteAttribute

NOTES:

Allows spectacular screen effects, e.g. Invert (GetBackground) causes inversion of the character and background colours.

restrictions on use: Text mode only.

3.22 Procedure Reverse

syntax: Reverse (color);

color is of the byte type.

function:

Gives the background at the current cursor position the colour of the character and the character the colour of the background.

pseudo-code:

a. read the character and its attribute
b. mask the attribute to preserve the blinking and double intensity bits
c. load bits 4 to 6 with color after loading bits 0 to 2 with the contents of bits 4 to 6
d. rewrite the character and its attribute.

mechanism:

As Invert.

listing:

```
procedure Reverse(color:byte);

const buffer : byte = $88;

begin
ReadScreen;
buffer:=buffer and attr;        {leaves character blinking or
                                 on high intensity}
attr:=(buffer or ((color and $07) shl 4)) or ((attr and $70)
SHR 4);
                                {swaps colours}
WriteAttribute(0,scrn_char,attr);
end;
```

declarations: Procedures ReadScreen, WriteAttribute.

NOTES:

Bits 3 and 7 are conserved. This means care has to be taken over the choice of colours.

restrictions on use: Text mode only.

3.23 Procedures InvertWord ReverseWord ColorWord.

Why not apply the above procedures to whole words? This would facilitate highlighting of titles or sections of menus on screen.

syntax: InvertWord (color);
ReverseWord (color);
ColorWord (color);

where color is of the byte type.

function

Applies procedures Invert, Reverse and Charcolor from the current cursor position up to the next blank space.

pseudo-code:

a. invert the current character
b. move the cursor on to the next position
c. read the character
d. test if it is a space.

listing:

```
procedure ColorWord(color:byte);

begin
repeat
CharColor(color);
GoNext;
ReadScreen;
until scrn_char = ' ';
GoPred;          {leaves the cursor under the last character}
end;

procedure InvertWord (color:byte);

begin
repeat
Invert(color);
GoNext;
ReadScreen;
until scrn_char = ' ';
GoPred;
end;

procedure ReverseWord (color:byte);
```

```
begin
repeat
Reverse(color);
GoNext;
ReadScreen;
until scrn_char = ' ';
GoPred;
end;
```

declarations: Invert, Reverse and CharColor and their declarations, GoNext.

NOTES:

It is easy to modify these procedures to produce HiliteWord, LoLiteWord, BlinkWord, etc....

Better still, you could write a single procedure, one of whose parameters would determine the function to apply to the word.

restrictions on use:

Text mode only.

3.24 Procedure GoNextWord

If we have waited until now to declare this cursor handling procedure it is because it uses ReadScreen and can be applied with the procedures above.

syntax: GoNextWord;

function:

Moves the cursor to the first non-space character after the end of the current word.

pseudo-code:

a. find the first space (end of current word)
b. look for the first non-space character (start of next word).

listing:

```
procedure GoNextWord;

begin
GetScreen;
CsrOff;
repeat                 {find the end of the current word}
GoNext;
ReadScreen;
until scrn_char = ' ';
while (scrn_char = ' ') and not((WhereX=colnum) and
(WhereY=25)) do
begin
```

```
GoNext;              {find the beginning of the next word}
ReadScreen;
end;
CsrOn;
end;
```

declarations: ReadScreen, GoNext, GetVideo [CsrOn, CsrOff?].

restrictions on use:

Text mode only.

CHAPTER 3

Text windows

1 ESSENTIAL INFORMATION

In the course of the last chapter we built up most of what we need for this chapter. There is just one standard text window management procedure in Turbo Pascal:

Window (x1, y1, x2, y2);

x1 and y1 define the top left-hand corner of the window and x2, y2 the bottom right-hand corner.

Remember that once this procedure has been called, any call to a procedure using screen coordinates will apply to the window above and the rest of the screen will be inaccessible until a full screen window is opened.

2 AIMS OF THIS CHAPTER

There is only one instruction available for handling windows efficiently. This may seem very little, but it is within the spirit of Pascal to provide the user with only the indispensable basic tools and to leave it to him to build up his own procedures according to his real needs. This is what we shall do here, remaining as simple as possible in our approach, creating routines of general value which will be easy to modify to meet the reader's requirements.

We shall learn in turn how we can:

—define a window permanently
—select a window by its number
—store a window in memory
—save the background on which we are working
—move a window, etc.

NB:

The procedures that we shall describe here form a coherent set and it will be difficult to use the routines described in this chapter on their own. All declarations are therefore important and we shall only mention the declarations to make beforehand if the procedures appear in another chapter.

3 PROCEDURES AND FUNCTIONS

Note:

These procedures use up memory space in proportion to the number of windows opened. Given the size of the buffers available, it is obvious that the maximum number of windows will be limited by the configuration of the system and the size of the application program.

Another way of handling these procedures is to use a pointer, so they are only allocated memory space when a window is selected. This way of proceeding, which is significantly more economical at the memory level, leads to complications in the writing of such procedures and in access to individual windows, which has to take place by means of chained lists (using the traditional method based on pointers).

In any case, programs in which it will be necessary to manage more than two or three windows at the same time will be rare, and in most cases it will be possible to use the simplified method proposed here.

3.1 Declarations and Procedure DefTextWindow

We shall start by defining the maximum number of windows we shall use. This has to be determined as a function of user requirements and memory size. The number is limited to three, by default, in the declaration of the constant nbwindows.

Let us now consider the first procedure.

syntax: DefTextWindow (number, x1, y1, x2, y2);

all parameters are of the byte type.

function:

Defines a window by establishing a correspondence between a window number (number) and a set of coordinates equivalent to those used by the Window instruction.

pseudo-code

a. load the four coordinates of the window into a two-dimensional array with the first dimension used for the window number.

listing:

```
const
nbwindows = 3;
{change this number if you are using more or less than 3
windows}

var
WinRefTable: array[1..nbwindows,1..4] of byte;

procedure DefTextWindow (number, x1, y1, x2, y2:byte);

begin
WinRefTable[number,1]:=x1;   {loads the coordinates of the}
WinRefTable[number,2]:=y1;   {window into the reference table}
WinRefTable[number,3]:=x2;
WinRefTable[number,4]:=y2;
end;
```

declarations: None.

NOTES:

This definition can be made once and for all (on condition you do not want to change the window size later). Number 0 is used for the full screen window.

restrictions on use:

Text mode only.

3.2 Procedure SelTextWindow

Having defined one or more windows, we now want to be able to use them. Rather than constantly calling a tiresome sequence of x and y coordinates, all we need do now is to call a predefined window by its number.

syntax: SelTextWindow (number);

number is of the byte type.

function:

Activates the window defined by number using procedure DefTextWindow.

Updates the variable ActiveWindow which indicates at any time which window is active.

Updates the variables XTextLimit and YTextLimit which represent the maximum coordinates usable within the window.

Selects the full screen window independently of the active text mode.

pseudo-code:

a. check the current screen mode
b. if calling window 0: full screen
c. else activate window number
d. update the number of the active window
e. update the limits of the usable screen (within the window)
f. set frame to false (see SelFramedWindow).

listing:

```
const

ActiveWindow    :    byte = 0;
XTextLimit      :    byte = 80;      {80 column mode by
default}
YTextLimit      :    byte = 25;
Frame            :    boolean = false;

procedure SelTextWindow(number:byte);

begin
GetScreen;
if number = 0  {if 0 then full screen}
```

```
then
begin
Window (1,1,colnum,25);
XTextLimit:=colnum;
YTextLimit:=25;
end
else
begin
Window (WinRefTable[number,1],WinRefTable[number,2],
       WinRefTable[number,3],WinRefTable[number,4]);

XTextLimit:=WinRefTable[number,3]-WinRefTable[number,1]+1;
YTextLimit:=WinRefTable[number,4]-WinRefTable[number,2]+1;
                              {screen limits}

Frame:=false;                 {used or frame protection}
end;
ActiveWindow:=number; {updates the number of the active
                       window}
                      {and the maximum values of coordinates}
end;
```

declarations: GetScreen, DefTextWindow.

NOTES:

Variable ActiveWindow is initialized to 0, which is natural since the program will always be entered in full screen mode.

restrictions on use: Text mode only.

3.3 Function TextWindowSelected

It is important to know at any time which window is active and which is not. This simple function plays a complementary role to variable Active Window.

syntax: TextWindowSelected(number);

number is of the byte type. The value returned is of the boolean type.

function:

Returns true if the active window is window *number*;

pseudo-code:

a. check the validity of the call
b. if OK compare the number called with the active number…
c. … and return the result of the comparison
d. else return false.

listing:

```
function TextWindowSelected(number:byte):boolean;

begin
if number in [0..nbwindows]
    then
        TextWindowSelected:=(ActiveWindow = number)
    else
        TextWindowSelected:=false;
end;
```

declarations: None.

NOTES: None.

restrictions on use: None.

3.4 Procedures GoNextWin and GoPredWin

GoNext and GoPred cannot be used in window mode as the screen limits have to be known. We have now defined them, so that we can complete our cursor management procedures. The limits on movement are automatically modified to be compatible with the active window.

syntax: GoNextWin;
GoPredWin;

function:
Same role as GoNext and GoPred, but the cursor moves logically within the window limits.

listing:

```
procedure GoNextWin;

begin

    if not (WhereX=XTextLimit)     {right hand limit ?}
        then
            GotoXY(Where X+1,WhereY)
        else
            If (WhereX=XTextLimit) and (WhereY=YTextLimit)
                                          {bottom of screen?}
        then
            GoToXY(1,1)
        else
            GoToXY(1,WhereY+1);
end;

procedure GoPredWin;
```

```
begin
    if not(WhereX=1)            {left hand limit?}
        then
            GoToXY(WhereX-1,WhereY)
        else
            If (WhereX=1) and (WhereY=1)   {top of screen?}
        then
            GoToXY(XTextLimit,YTextLimit)
        else
            GoToXY(XTextLimit,WhereY-1);
end;
```

declarations: None.

NOTES:

The call to GetScreen will have to take place beforehand and must always be valid if the program is not to behave erratically.

restrictions on use: Text mode only.

3.5 Procedure KeepTextWindow and Declaration of Window Buffers

Having selected a window and filled it with interesting information, it may be a pity to lose its contents. Again, the window may have been opened on an area whose contents were of importance and needed to be saved. KeepTextWindow solves these problems.

syntax: KeepTextWindow (act, object);

act is of the action type	=	(load, save)
object is of the obj type	=	(window, background).

function:

Depending on the value of act (load or save), this procedure loads or saves the contents of the active window in the buffer defined by object, which may take one of the values window and background.

This dry explanation hides a very simple form of operation. Let us take an example or two:

KeepTextWindow (save, window) has the effect of saving the contents of the active window, under its number, in the buffer set aside for holding window contents.

KeepTextWindow (load,background) has the effect of restoring to the screen the original contents of the background on which the window was opened (on condition that it was previously saved using KeepTextWindow (save, background)).

act	=	save	=> save
act	=	load	=> restore
object	=	window	=> uses the window buffer
object	=	background	=> uses the background buffer

pseudo-code:

a. if act = save...
   a1. for all logical positions in the window...
   a2 ... read the character and its attriubte...
   a3. and save them in the buffer selected
b. if act = load...
   b1. for all logical positions in the window...
   b2. extract the character and attribute from the selected buffer...
   b3. and display them.

mechanism:

The important part of this procedure is the use of ReadScreen to obtain data from the screen and WriteAttribute to restore them to it. GoNext is not used to scan the screen as this procedure would be too slow here.

listing:

```
const textwindowsize = 2000;  {set according to needs}

type
action      =     (save, load);
obj         =     (window,background);

var

WindowBuffer:  array[1..2,1..nbwindows,1..textwindowsize]of
byte;

procedure KeepTextWindow(choice:action;object:obj);

var

bufindex,col,row     :    byte;
counter              :    integer;

begin

CsrOff;
SelTextWindow(ActiveWindow);          {careful if a frame}
counter:=1;
bufindex:=Ord(object)+1;

case choice of
save:                   {for all characters in the window...}
for row:=1 to YTextLimit do
for col:=1 to XTextLimit do

begin
GoToXY (col,row);
```

```
ReadScreen;     {reads the character and attribute at the
                 cursor position}

WindowBuffer[bufindex,ActiveWindow,counter]:=ord(scrn_char);
WindowBuffer[bufindex,ActiveWindow,counter+1]:=attr;
counter:=counter+2;
                {and loads them into the buffer selected.}
end;

load:           {for all position in the window...}
for row:=1 to YTextLimit do
for col:=1 to XTextLimit do

begin
    {writes the character and attribute contained in the
     buffer}
GoToXY(col,row);
WriteAttribute(0,
chr(WindowBuffer[bufindex,ActiveWindow,counter]),
WindowBuffer[bufindex,ActiveWindow,counter+1]);
counter:=counter+2;
end;
end;        {of case}

CsrOn;
end;
```

declarations: CsrOn, CsrOff, ReadScreen, WriteAttribute.

NOTES:

The WindowBuffer contains two arrays of 2000 bytes for each window number (window and background).

This buffer can only contain a half screen page (in 80 column mode) per window. If larger windows need to be saved, an array larger than the 2000 bytes provided has to be declared.

The option makes it possible to use various buffers, one for windows and the other for original screens.

To save the whole screen, rather than creating a large buffer, it is better to use procedure CopyPage (but this needs the graphics board).

restrictions on use: Text mode only.

3.6 Procedure ChangeTextWindow

To make handling of window contents still more flexible, we also need a facility to exchange data between buffers and the active window. ChangeTextWindow handles this task.

syntax: ChangeTextWindow (object);

object is of the obj type.

function:

Exchanges the contents of the active window for the contents of the window or background buffer.

pseudo-code:

a. for each logical position in the window...
b. read the character from the screen and place it in a save buffer (one byte)
c. display the corresponding character from the selected buffer (window or background)
d. place the character saved in the freed slot in the buffer.

mechanism:

The procedure has to use two one-byte buffers to save the code and attribute of the character at the current cursor position each time the screen is read, since the corresponding slot in the buffer will only be freed once the substitute character is displayed.

listing:

```
procedure ChangeTextWindow(object:obj);

var

bufindex,col,row,
char_buffer,att_buffer    :    byte;
counter                   :    integer;

begin

SelTextWindow(ActiveWindow);
counter:=1;
bufindex:=Ord(object)+1;

{for all characters in the window}

for row:=1 to YTextLimit do
for col:=1 to XTextLimit do
begin
GoToXY (col,row);    {reads the character at the cursor
                      position}
ReadScreen;

WriteAttribute(0,
chr(WindowBuffer[bufindex,ActiveWindow,counter]),
WindowBuffer[bufindex,ActiveWindow,counter+1]);
WindowBuffer[bufindex,ActiveWindow,counter]:=ord(scrn_char);
WindowBuffer[bufindex,ActiveWindow,counter+1]:=attr;
```

```
counter:=counter+2;
end;        {... and replaces it with one from the buffer
             selected}
            {and stores it in the window buffer}
end;
```

declarations: ReadScreen, WriteAttribute, KeepTextWindow.

NOTES:

The instruction SelTextWindow (ActiveWindow), which may seem totally useless, in fact makes it possible to protect against the effect of procedure SelFramedWindow which, if it has been used, will have reduced the size of the window but without changing its references. (See below.)

The same is true for KeepTextWindow and MoveTextWindow.

restrictions on use: Text mode only.

3.7 Procedure MoveTextWindow

As we now know how to save window data, save original screens and restore data from background and window buffers, we now have all the tools necessary to move the window of our choice to anywhere on the screen.

syntax: MoveTextWindow (deltax, deltay);

deltax and detay are of the integer type.

function:

Moves the active window by deltax and deltay, expressed as a number of lines and columns, updating the coordinates of the window in the reference table and ensuring that screen limits are observed.

pseudo-code:

a. test the display mode and the validity of the requested displacement
b. if not valid, correct deltax and deltay
c. save the contents of the window and restore the original background
d. define the new window
e. select it
f. save the new background and display the window contents again.

mechanism:

All we do is use the four procedures defined above. The trick is to redefine the coordinates of a new window whose coordinates are the same as the old one's except that they have been increased or decreased by deltax or deltay.

listing:

```
procedure MoveTextWindow(deltax,deltay:integer);
```

```
var
newx1,newx2,newy1,newy2: integer;

begin
CsrOff;
SelTextWindow(ActiveWindow);        {precaution in case of
                                     frame}
GetScreen;      {tests whether screen coordinates have
                 been exceeded}
                {if yes, recalculate displacement.}

if (WinRefTable[ActiveWindow,1]+deltax <1)          then
                 deltax:=1-WinRefTable[ActiveWindow,1];
if (WinRefTable[ActiveWindow,2]+deltay <1)          then
                 deltay:=1-WinRefTable[ActiveWindow,2];
if (WinRefTable[ActiveWindow,3]+deltax >colnum)     then
                 deltax:=colnum-WinRefTable[ActiveWindow,3];
if (WinRefTable[ActiveWindow,4]+deltay >25)         then
                 deltay:=25-WinRefTable[ActiveWindow,4];

ChangeTextWindow(background);       {save the window and}
                                    {load the original
                                     background}

newx1:=WinRefTable[ActiveWindow,1]+deltax;
newx2:=WinRefTable[ActiveWindow,3]+deltax;
newy1:=WinRefTable[ActiveWindow,2]+deltay;
newy2:=WinRefTable[ActiveWindow,4]+deltay; {redefines the
                                            window}

DefTextWindow(ActiveWindow,newx1,newy1,newx2,newy2);

SelTextWindow(ActiveWindow);                {selects the
                                             new window.}
ChangeTextWindow(background);  {saves the new background and
                                reloads the window}
CsrOn;

end;
```

declarations: ReadScreen, WriteAttribute, CsrOn, CsrOff.

NOTES:

The background corresponding to the starting position of the window is assumed to have been saved using procedure KeepTextWindow (save, background).

This comment only applies to the first displacement. For any later displacements, such saving is automatic.

The displacement time will grow with the size of the window. On the other hand it is independent distance since the displacement does not take place by sliding but by a direct jump.

restrictions on use: Text mode only.

3.8 Procedure FrameTextWindow

The reader will undoubtedly have noticed that the fact that a window has been selected produces no change on the screen. Physically, nothing makes the window visible. It will often therefore be necessary to frame the window selected. This leads to a small problem:

—If the window is framed from outside (technique used in the WINDOWS.PAS demonstration program in the Turbo Pascal package), it cannot be moved;

—If it is framed from inside, there is a problem when scrolling within a frame drawn at the outer edges of the screen. However, we know from the work we did in the previous chapter (procedure Box) how to solve this problem. We simply have to adapt the procedure to the window context.

syntax: FrameTextWindow (color, line);

color and line are of the byte type.

function:

Automatically draws a frame of the size of the window, in colour color and using single or double lines depending on the value of line.

pseudo-code:

See procedure Box.

mechanism:

Here the mechanism for calculating the memory position of the bottom right-hand corner of the window is a little less simple than in procedure Box.

Furthermore, a definite segment is defined for the beginning of the screen memory depending on whether a monochrome or colour configuration is being used. See the description of the screen memory organization in text mode for an explanation of why this is so.

listing:

```
procedure FrameTextWindow(color,line:byte);

const

FrameChar:   array[1..2,1..6] of char =

((#218,#191,#192,#217,#196,#179),

(#201,#187,#200,#188,#205,#186));

var

i,pos,base,offset:integer;
```

```
begin
GetScreen;               {identical mechanism as for procedure
                          Box}
CsrOff;                  {see the procedures in the section on
                          screen.prc}
SelTextWindow(ActiveWindow);
TextColor(color);

gotoXY(1,1);write(FrameChar[line,1]);
for i:=2 to XTextLimit-1 do write (FrameChar[line,5]);
write(FrameChar[line,2]);
for i:=2 to YTextLimit-1 do

begin
gotoXY(1,i);write(FrameChar[line,6]);
gotoXY(XTextLimit,i);
write(FrameChar[line,6]);
end;

gotoXY(1,YTextLimit);
write(FrameChar[line,3]);

for i:=2 to XTextLimit-1
         do write(FrameChar[line,5]);

pos:=     (WinRefTable[ActiveWindow,3] + {calculate position
                                          of bottom}
           WinRefTable[ActiveWindow,4] - 1) * colnum;
                                         {right-hand corner}

if screen_mode=7         {monochrome?}
then
base:=$B000
else
base:=$B800;

Mem[base:(2 * pos) - 2] := ord (FrameChar[line,4]);
{right bottom left-hand corner character}

Mem[base:((2 * pos) - 2) + 1]:= Mem[base:((2 * pos) -2) -1];
{same attribute as preceding character}

CsrOn;

end;
```

declarations: GetScreen, CsrOn, CsrOff.

NOTES: None.

restrictions on use: Text mode only.

3.9 Procedure SelFramedWindow

The presence of a frame around the window makes its handling friendlier, but steps must be taken to avoid any sudden displacement of the screen or inadequately controlled attempts to write to it. This is provided for simply by the following procedure.

syntax: SelFramedWindow;

function:
Stores the frame of the active window and selects the window immediately within it.

listing:

```
procedure SelFramedWindow;

begin

Window(WinRefTable[ActiveWindow,1]+1,
WinRefTable[ActiveWindow,2]+1,
WinRefTable[ActiveWindow,3]-1,WinRefTable[ActiveWindow,4]-1);
XTextLimit:=XTextLimit-2;
YTextLimit:=YTextLimit-2;
Frame:=true;         {precaution for scrolling}

end;
```

declarations: None.

NOTES:

The size of the window is reduced by two characters along each axis.

This saving operation is nullified by: KeepTextWindow
MoveTextWindow
SelTextWindow
FrameTextWindow.

The boolean variable Frame is updated to ensure that procedure Scroll operates correctly.

restrictions on use: Text mode only.

3.10 Procedure ScrollWindow

This procedure is a modified form of procedure Scroll, which we examined in the previous chapter, adapted to window handling. It also reads variable Frame, updated by procedure FrameTextWindow, in order to ensure that scrolling only takes place in the usable area of the window.

syntax: ScrollWindow (direction, linecount, attribute);

direction is of boolean type,
linecount and attribute are of integer type.

function:

Scrolls the window upwards or downwards, according to whether direction is true or false, by a number of lines equal to linecount and assigning the attribute specified by attribute to the space characters used as filling.

NB:

If linecount is equal to 0, the whole window is cleared.

pseudo-code:

a. if the window is framed, allow for the necessary difference in area
b. call procedure Scroll, passing the coordinates of the active window to it.

listing:

```
procedure
ScrolWindow(direction:boolean;linecount,attribute:integer);

var

protect:byte;

begin

if frame then protect:=1 else protect:=0;     {protect
                                determines whether or not}
Scroll(direction,                 {the whole window is scrolling}
linecount,                        {or just the frame}
attribute,
WinRefTable[ActiveWindow,1]+protect,
WinRefTable[ActiveWindow,2]+protect,
WinRefTable[ActiveWindow,3]-protect,
WinRefTable[ActiveWindow,4]-protect);

end;
```

declarations: Procedure Scroll.

NOTES: None.

restrictions on use: Text mode only.

CHAPTER 4

Graphics

1 ESSENTIAL INFORMATION

We have already examined the fundamental concepts used in graphics modes. As in text modes, the structure of the screen memory is easy to understand. On the other hand, its handling is far less simple given that a point is not represented by a byte but by one or two bits, i.e. there are eight or four points per byte. Though addressing these points on screen is made very easy by the use of basic BIOS services and standard Turbo Pascal routines, it is clear that we will not be able to handle the display as simply as we did in text mode in the chapter concerned with display.

1.1 Use of memory

In graphics mode almost all the screen memory is used. In fact, there are two free areas of 192 bytes which are unused and only provide an alignment zone at paragraph starts (a paragraph is a 16-byte memory area).

It is important to bear in mind that, unlike the memory image of text mode characters, the various points (pixels) are not represented continuously but held as lines (odd and even lines) in two different zones in memory.

Let us consider this in detail.

In medium resolution mode there are 320 × 200 points to represent, i.e. 64 000 points. The available memory is 16K i.e. 131 072 bits, allowing two bits per point (and therefore four colours). The first memory block, from 0 to 8K, contains all even screen lines from 0 to 198 and 192 free bytes, and the second block begins at the 8K border and contains 100 odd lines from 1 to 199 followed by a final 192-byte space.

This memory organization becomes apparent if, for example, a BASIC BLOAD is executed in screen memory of a graphics file. First the even lines appear, 'cross-hatching' the screen, and then the image is completed using the odd lines. This phenomenon will be eliminated when we study procedures for saving and restoring graphics screens.

Each point is consequently represented by two bits which define its colour (0 for the background colour and 1 to 3 for colours from the range selected). Two colour palettes are normally available, but Turbo Pascal allows four by making use of Port 3D9H.

The particular way in which screen memory is divided up in graphics mode prevents our using simple display handling procedures.

1.2 Character representation

A request to write a character on screen in graphics mode causes the system to consult a table in which the 128 basic characters are stored and then draw one on the screen. In this standard case, access is not normally possible to the full 256 characters available in text mode. To allow such access, a call has to be issued to the DOS command GRAPHTABL before the program is executed.

The graphic representation of the character uses an 8×8 point matrix. This has one immediate consequence: since there are 320 points per line in medium resolution mode we can only display 40 columns of characters (as opposed to 80 in high resolution).

The display coordinates of the characters are the same as in text mode, which is reasonably convenient. We shall write a little function which allows us to establish the correspondence between a pixel position and a character position.

A useful piece of information is that procedure Pattern also uses an 8×8 matrix to define the fill patter for an area. Why should we not use it to define our own characters?

It should simply be noted that the pattern will be represented in reverse order, compared with the order of bytes entered through procedure pattern (this is something not specified in the Turbo Pascal manual).

1.3 Absolute coordinates

The only coordinates recognized by the system at the basic service level are absolute screen coordinates. The coordinates of the upper left-hand corner of the screen are always 0,0 and those of the bottom right-hand corner are either 319, 199 or 639, 199. This type of representation is not particularly friendly and one of our aims will be to improve it. It must, however, be borne in mind that this type of coordinate is the only kind recognised by the standard or extended graphics procedures in Turbo Pascal.

1.4 Graphics windows

Their behaviour is exactly the same as that of text windows. When a window is activated, the coordinate system refers to the upper left-hand corner of the window and no longer to that of the screen, but all the other comments above remain valid.

2 AIMS OF THIS CHAPTER

The standard Turbo Pascal graphics procedures are efficient but always governed by the general philosophy of the language, i.e. they are limited to absolutely indispensable tools, in order not to overload the library of basic routines unnecessarily.

We shall therefore attempt throughout this chapter to make our life somewhat easier by building up a number of utilities for which the guiding themes will be the following:

—definition of user coordinate systems
—use of these systems and conversion procedures
—definition and selection of windows
—movement of windows
—screen memory or window handling
—saving screen images or windows on file.

It has to be clearly understood that we are not attempting to build up a graphics management system as efficient as the Turbo Graphix Toolbox, but simply to show that with a few reasonably short procedures it is possible to simplify programming work considerably.

The procedures studied can be applied in both graphics modes. In this chapter, even more than in the others, it is quite out of the question to isolate the procedures proposed from each other. In any case, most declarations of variables will be made, for practical reasons, in the first procedure. Any attempt to isolate one routine from the other will have to take careful account of all the necessary declarations. As in the chapter dealing with windows, only declarations of procedures drawn from other chapters will be mentioned here.

Warning:

Graphics windows consume even more memory than text windows: 8000 bytes per window (adjustable default value) and 16 000 bytes for the screen buffer.

The comments made concerning text windows also apply here.

The default mode is medium resolution. To obtain correct operation of high resolution procedures (in particular coordinate conversion functions), window 0 will have to have been activated at least once in order to change the full screen references.

Procedures for moving windows and for merging buffers or patterns require version 3.0 of Turbo Pascal.

3 PROCEDURES AND FUNCTIONS

Before starting our description of the various routines in the chapter, we shall move directly to the necessary declarations. This will not be our general approach in this book, but in this particular case the various procedures are too interdependent for their declarations to be made as we move through the various explanations.

3.1 Declarations

Constants:

nbworlds:

This constant represents the number of user coordinate systems you want to hold in memory. There is no particular limit to this number. We will assign value five to it by default.

World is the usual name for a user coordinate system.

nbgraphwindows:

This is the maximum number of windows you can manage simmultaneously using the procedures we shall describe here.

nbpatterns:

This is the maximum number of different patterns that can be made available to you in memory through variable PatternLib.

graphwindowsize:

This is the maximum size of a window, set at 8000 bytes by default. It is up to you to adjust the value depending on what is possible within your own system.

XGraphLimit and YGraphLimit:

These constants are initialized to 319 and 199 and give the maximum values for the absolute x- and y-coordinates of a point whatever the active mode. These values are modified by the formation of a window and then represent the maximum values of x- and y-coordinates within that window.

ActiveGraphWindow:

This constant with type byte and intialized to 0 (full screen) makes it possible to find out at any time what the number of the last activated window is.

XWorldRatio and YWorldRatio:

This gives the ratio between the limiting values of screen coordinates of the active window and the maximum interval in the active world system. That value is set to one by default.

Types:

OneWindowBuffer:

As its name suggests, this type of variable makes it possible to store a graphics window or 8000 bytes by default. To handle windows larger than half a screen, it is simply necessary to change the value of graphwindowsize.

PolyWindowBuffer:

An array of OneWindowBuffer.

HalfScreen:

An array of 8000 bytes allowing the whole screen to be handled in halves (problem of even and odd lines described above).

Patt:

Eight-byte array used for pattern handling.

Variables:

WorldRefTable:

Two-dimensional array containing the minimum and maximum values of user coordinates along each axis for every number in the coordinate system.

GraphWinRefTable:

Two-dimensional array containing the coordinates of the top left-hand and bottom right-hand corners of each window number.

GraphScreenBuffer:

Makes it possible to store an entire screen in memory.

HalfScreen1 and HalfScreen2:

Absolute address variables representing the two useful parts of screen memory (Halfscreen1 for even lines and Halfscreen2 for odd lines).

GraphWindowBuffer: Window storage buffer.

ActiveWorld : Number of the active coordinate system.

Xinterval:

Yinterval:

Width and height respectively of the active user coordinate system.

PatternLib:

Library of patterns usable by Fillpattern and FillWindowPattern.

ActivePattern: Number of the active pattern.

listing:

```
const

    nbworlds = 5;
    {this number should be changed if more or less than 5
     worlds are being used}

    nbgraphwindows = 3;
    {this number should be changed if more or less than 3
     windows are being used}
    {increases in this number are limited by the system's
     memory capacity}

    nbpatterns = 5;
    graphwindowsize = 8000;

    Ygraphlimit : integer = 199;
    Xgraphlimit : integer = 319;
    ActiveGraphWindow : byte = 0;
    XWorldRatio : real = 1;
    YWorldRatio : real = 1;

type

OneWindowBuffer = array[1..graphwindowsize] of byte;
PolyWindowBuffer = array[1..nbgraphwindows] of
OneWindowBuffer;
HalfScreen = array[0..7999] OF byte;
patt = array[0..7] of byte;

var

WorldRefTable : array[1..nbworlds,1..4] of real;
GraphWinRefTable: array[1..nbgraphwindows,1..4] of integer;
GraphScreenBuffer : array[1..2] of HalfScreen;

HalfScreen1: HalfScreen absolute $B800:0;
HalfScreen2: HalfScreen absolute $B800:$2000;
```

```
GraphWindowBuffer: PolyWindowBuffer;
PatternLib: array[1..nbpatterns] of patt;
ActiveWorld,
ActivePattern : byte;
Xinterval,
Yinterval, real;
```

3.2 Procedure DefWorld

As we said above, it is inconvenient to work in terms of absolute screen coordinates if only because it is fairly difficult to plan graphs with the y-axis reversed. It is also essential not to have to go through the calculations needed to convert relative to absolute coordinates. This is the aim of this procedure and the functions which follow it.

syntax: Defworld (number,xmin,ymin,xmax,ymax);

number is of type byte,
coordinates are of type real.

function:

Defines the upper and lower limits of the user coordinate system identified by number.

E.g.: If you want to work in a coordinate system whose limits are –1500 and +750 on the x-axis and +350 and +970 on the y-axis (why not after all?) simply enter:

DefWorld (reference number, –1500, 350, 750, 970);

listing:

```
procedure DefWorld (number:byte;xmin,ymin,xmax,ymax:real);

begin
WorldRefTable[number,1]:=xmin;      {loads the coordinate}
WorldRefTable[number,2]:=ymin;      {limits into the}
WorldRefTable[number,3]:=xmax;      {reference table}
WorldRefTable[number,4]:=ymax;
end;
```

NOTES: None.

3.3 Procedure SelWorld

To work in a given coordinate system, and to ensure that the conversion procedures operate correctly, they have to know what references they are to use.

syntax: SelWorld (number);

number is of the byte type.

function:

Activates the coordinate system defined by number. Nothing actually happens except that the references for procedures Xw and Yw are modified.

listing:

```
procedure SelWorld(number:byte);

begin
if number in [1.. nbworlds] then
begin
ActiveWorld:=number;

Xinterval:=WorldRefTable[number,3]-WorldRefTable[number,1]+1;
Yinterval:=WorldRefTable[number,4]-WorldRefTable[number,2]+1;
{width and height of world}

XWorldRatio:=(XGraphLimit+1) / Xinterval;
YWorldRatio:=(YGraphLimit+1) / Yinterval;
{ratio of dimensions to screen or window coordinates}

end;
end;
```

NOTES:

Detailed comments are no more necessary for this procedure than for the preceding one.

Updating of XWorldRatio and YWorldRatio allows use of the coordinate conversion function defined below.

3.4 Conversion functions Xw and Yw

Once the user coordinate system has been defined, coordinates expressed in this new system have to be converted into absolute screen coordinates if any of the standard graphics procedures are to be used. This is the role of Xw and Yw (where w stands for world).

syntax: Xw (x)
Yw (y);

x and y are of real type. The value returned is of integer type.

function:

Converts the real number x or y expressed as world coordinates into an integer compatible with screen coordinates and those of the active window.

pseudo-code:

a. calculate the difference between the coordinates of the point and the minimum coordinate of the axis in question in the selected world system.

b. multiply that difference by the ratio between the maximum number of addressable points on that axis and the maximum interval, along that axis, within the system defined by the user. This ratio is updated by procedure Selworld under label XWorldRatio or YWorldRatio.

mechanism:

We shall take an example to see how this procedure works.

If we are in medium resolution graphics mode, there are 320 addressable points along the x-axis (in full screen mode).

Assume the user has defined a system with the following limits:

xmin = 0
ymin = 0
xmax = 1000
ymax = 1000.

In this system, we want to plot a point whose x-coordinate is 500.

Its difference from the minimum is 500 – 0 = 500.

The maximum interval along that axis is 1001.

The point would be plotted at coordinate $x = 500 \times 320 / 1001 = 160$, which is indeed the central position in the interval.

listing:

```
function Xw(x:real):integer;

begin
Xw:=abs(Round((x-WorldRefTable[ActiveWorld,1]) *
XWorldRatio));
end;

function Yw(y:real):integer;

begin
Yx:=abs(Round((WorldRefTable[ActiveWorld,4]-y) *
YWorldRatio));
end;
```

declarations: None.

NOTES: The calculation inverts the values on the y-axis.

restrictions on use: None.

3.5 Conversion functions Pc and Cp

It is sometimes important, when mixing text and graphics, to find out what absolute screen coordinate corresponds to a particular character position expressed in terms of lines and columns. The following two functions make it easy to establish this correspondence, in either direction.

syntax: Pc (c)
Cp (p);

c and p are of integer type. The values returned are of integer type.

function:

Pc gives the x- or y-coordinates of the bottom right hand pixel of the character matrix at line or column c.

Cp gives the line or column of the character whose matrix includes the pixel with coordinate p.

mechanism:

This calculation is based on the fact that a character always occupies eight pixels along both axes. It is therefore independent of the current axes and graphics mode.

listing:

```
function Cp(p:integer):integer;

begin
if p>=0 then Cp:=p div 8 + 1 else Cp:=1;
end;

function Pc(c:integer):integer;

begin
if c>=1 then Pc:=c * 8 - 1 else Pc:=0;
end;
```

declarations: None.

NOTES:

This function is very useful if we want to place some text at a specific point on a graph if we do not know its coordinates in advance.

restrictions on use: None.

3.6 Procedure DefGraphWindow

We shall make no comment on this procedure whose mechanism is identical to that for text windows.

syntax: DefGraphWindow (number, x1, y1, x2, y2);

number is of the byte type. Coordinates are of the integer type.

function:

Defines a graphics window.

listing:

```
procedure DefGraphWindow(number,x1,y1,x2,y2:integer);

begin
```

```
GraphWinRefTable[number,1]:=x1;      {as for text windows}
GraphWinRefTable[number,2]:=y1;
GraphWinRefTable[number,3]:=x2;
GraphWinRefTable[number,4]:=y2;

end;
```

declarations: None.

restrictions on use: None.

3.7 Procedure SelGraphWindow

This operation is a little more cumbersome in graphics mode than in text mode as a certain number of constants have to be updated.

In principle, however, the operation is exactly the same.

syntax: SelGraphWindow (number);

number is of byte type.

function:

(i) Activates the window specified by number.
(ii) Allows a change to full screen mode taking account of the current graphics mode.
(iii) Updates the limiting values of the coordinates of the window or
(iv) the full screen ready for use by other functions.
(v) Updates the number of the active window.

pseudo-code:

a. test the screen mode
b. if number = 0...
   b1. update the screen limits
   b2. activate the full screen window in the current mode
c. else if the number is valid...
   c1. activate the window
   c2. update constants.

mechanism:

Nothing out of the ordinary, except the use of a function declared as external to calculate the maximum x-coordinate for full screen mode.

listing:

```
function XModeLimit:integer;  {determines the maximum x
                               coordinate}
                              {also used for window}
begin                          {movements}
GetScreen;
```

```
case screen_mode of
4..5 : XModeLimit:=319;
   6 : XModeLimit:=639;
end;
end;

procedure SelGraphWindow(number:byte);

begin

case number of                {full screen window}
     0 :  begin
          XGraphLimit:=XModeLimit;
          YGraphLimit:=199;
          GraphWindow(0,0,XGraphLimit,199);
          ActiveGraphWindow:=0;
          end;

1..nbgraphwindows: begin

GraphWindow(GraphWinRefTable[number,1],GraphWinRefTable
[number,2],
          GraphWinRefTable[number,3],GraphWinRefTable
[number,4]);

XGraphLimit:=GraphWinRefTable[number,3]-
GraphWinRefTable[number,1];
YGraphLimit:=GraphWinRefTable[number,4]-
GraphWinRefTable[number,2];
{new screen limits}

ActiveGraphWindow:=number;

end;
end;
end;
```

declarations: Procedure GetScreen.

NOTES:

XGraphLimit takes the value 319 at the start of program execution. If we move directly into high resolution mode we have to activate window 0, even if we are already in the full screen mode.

Function XModeLimit is declared as an external function as it will also be used for managing window movements.

restrictions on use: None.

3.8 Function GraphWindowSelected

We sometimes need to know which the active window is. This function provides that information.

syntax: GraphWindowSelected (number);

number is of byte type the value returned is of boolean type.

function:

Returns true if window number is active.

pseudo-code:

a. test the validity of number
b. compare number with the number of the active window
c. if different, or not valid, return false.

listing:

```
function GraphWindowSelected(number:byte):boolean;
begin
if number in [0..nbGraphwindows]
    then
        GraphWindowSelected:=(number = ActiveGraphWindow)
    else
        GraphWindowSelected:=false;
end;
```

declarations: None.

NOTES: None.

restrictions on use: None.

3.9 Procedure DrawWorldAxis

Drawing the coordinate axes is always a tedious operation. It is even more complicated if we are using world coordinates. Here is a simplified axis-plotting procedure which can be improved as necessary later.

syntax:

DrawWorldAxis (offsetx, offsety, xaside, yaside, stepx, stepy, xmark, ymark, color);

all parameters are of integer type.

function:

Plot two perpendicular axes, x and y, crossing at world coordinates offsetx and offsety.

In the case of axes crossing close to the bottom left-hand corner of the screen or window, it is likely we shall want to reserve a little space for text. Xaside and yaside will be used to allow this gap. The value will have to be taken into account in defining our coordinate system.

A scale mark will be drawn at intervals stepx along the x-axis and stepy along the y-axis, and the size of the interval is determined by xmark and ymark respectively.

All these values are assumed to be expressed in the coordinates of the active world.

The axes and scale marks will be drawn in colour color.

pseudo-code:

a. procedure DrawAxis
   a1. add the offsets and intervals to the basic coordinates of the axes
   a2. draw the axes
b. procedure DrawMark
   b1. evaluate the number of marks to draw
   b2. draw a mark
   b3. increment the coordinates by the step requested
   b4. draw the next mark...

mechanism:

Straightforward use of the standard procedure Draw.

listing:

```
procedure DrawWorldAxis(offsetx,offsety,
                        xaside, yaside,
                        stepx, stepy,
                        xmark, ymark,
                        color     :integer);

procedure Drawaxis;       {subroutine: plotting axes}

begin
Draw(Xw(WorldRefTable[ActiveWorld,1]+xaside),
Yw(WorldRefTable[ActiveWorld,2]+offsety),
Xw(WorldRefTable[ActiveWorld,3]),
Yw(WorldRefTable[ActiveWorld,2]+offsety),
color);
Draw(Xw(WorldRefTable[ActiveWorld,1]+offsetx),
Yw(WorldRefTable[ActiveWorld,2]+yaside),
Xw(WorldRefTable[ActiveWorld,1]+offsetx),
Yw(WorldRefTable[ActiveWorld,4]),
color);

end;

procedure Drawmark; {subroutine:  drawing marks}

var

    i:integer;

begin
    for i:=1 to Trunc (Xinterval /stepx) do
```

```
draw(Xw(WorldRefTable[ActiveWorld,1] + offsetx + stepx * i),
Yw(WorldRefTable[ActiveWorld,2] + offsety),
Xw(WorldRefTable[ActiveWorld,1] + offsetx + stepx * i),
Yw(WorldRefTable[ActiveWorld,2] + offsety + xmark),
color);

for i:=1 to Trunc (Yinterval / stepy) do

draw (Xw(WorldRefTable[ActiveWorld,1] + offsetx),
Yw(WorldRefTable[ActiveWorld,2] + offsety + stepy * i),
Xw(WorldRefTable[ActiveWorld,1] + offsetx + ymark),
Yw(worldRefTable[ActiveWorld,2] + offsety + stepy * i),
color);

end;

begin

    DrawAxis;
    DrawMark;
end;
```

declarations: None.

NOTES:

Xaside and yaside truncate axes by the value specified. This has to be taken into account when defining the coordinate system world.

For example, if we want to use axes running from 0 to 100 but leaving space for axis labels, every five units, and our axes are to cross at 0,0, we define a world that is rather larger than necessary:

DefWorld(n, –5, –5, 100, 100);

To have the axes specified above we need:

DrawWorldAxis (0, 0, 5, 5, stepx, stepy, xmark, ymark, color);

We recommend that axes should not be defined at screen or window limits (offsetx, offsety, xaside and yaside should not all be equal to 0). Since the conversion functions Xw and Yw use function Round, the result might put the axis just outside the window, in which case it will not be drawn.

restrictions on use: None.

3.10 Procedures InitScreenBuffer and InitGraphWindowBuffer

The screen and window buffers are not necessarily empty when we start running a program. These initialization procedures will set those buffers to 0.

syntax: InitScreenBuffer;
InitGraphWindowBuffer;

function:

Resets buffers to 0. For window buffers, only the active window is affected.

mechanism:

Uses the standard procedure FillChar.

listing:

```
procedure InitScreenBuffer;

begin
    Fillchar(GraphScreenBuffer,SizeOf(GraphScreenBuffer),0);
end;

procedure InitGraphWindowBuffer;

begin
   if not GraphWindowSelected(0) {nothing to do if window =
                                   full screen}
   then
    FillChar(GraphWindowBuffer[ActiveGraphWindow],
    graphwindowsize,0);
end;
```

declarations: None.

NOTES: None.

restrictions on use: None.

3.11 Procedures KeepGraphScreen and ShowGraphScreen

In graphics mode, all screen memory is filled. There can therefore be no question of saving useful screens in various screen pages. We have to create our own buffer for any graphics screen we would rather not have to redraw.

syntax: KeepGraphScreen;
ShowGraphScreen;

function:

(i) KeepGraphScreen:
Saves the currently displayed screen to the buffer GraphScreenBuffer.

(ii) ShowGraphScreen:
Almost immediately displays the contents of the screen buffer.

mechanism:

The procedure operates entirely at the level of declarations and variables with absolute addresses HalfScreen1 and HalfScreen2. We simply have to assign these variables to the corresponding buffer, or, conversely, assign the contents of the buffer to the screen memory.

This operation is very rapid, far more rapid than programmed transfer by means of a loop. We have already used this technique in the chapter concerned with display, for handling screen pages.

listing:

```
procedure KeepGraphScreen;

begin
    GraphScreenBuffer[1]:=HalfScreen1; {transfer to the
                                        memory buffer}
    GraphScreenBuffer[2]:=HalfScreen2;
end;

procedure ShowScreenBuffer;

begin
HalfScreen1:=GraphScreenBuffer[1]; {transfer towards screen
                                    memory}
HalfScreen2:=GraphScreenBuffer[2];
end;
```

declarations: None.

NOTES:

Assignment by half screens has two advantages:

It saves space used in screen memory (2 × 192 bytes) and allows even and odd lines to be handled separately, making it possible to handle the following procedure more elegantly.

restrictions on use: None.

3.12 Procedure ChangeGraphScreen

Procedure ShowScreenBuffer is rapid but has the disadvantage that it clears the screen currently displayed. If that screen also needs to be saved, use ChangeGraphScreen.

syntax: ChangeGraphScreen (direction);

direction is of direction type = (up, down, left, right).

function:

Exchanges the contents of the screen buffer with the screen currently being displayed.

The side by which the new screen appears is determined by the value of direction. The possible options are: up, down, left and right.

pseudo-code:

a. if the direction is up or down (work line by line)...
  a1. for each pair of screen lines...
  a2. calculate the offset of the first byte for the even line and the odd line respectively
  a3. store the corresponding bytes from the buffer in a temporary one-byte buffer
  a4. load the screen buffer with the corresponding byte from the screen memory
  a5. load the screen memory with the contents of the temporary one-byte buffer
  a6 move to the next byte
b. if the option is left or right
  ... same mechanism, but column by column.

mechanism:

The replacement loops for each byte are listed to two levels for up and down and to three levels for left and right.

In both cases, the final level ensures switching between even and odd lines by adding an offset of $2000, or 8192 bytes. Calculating offset1 and offset2 beforehand for each loop leads to a significant saving in time, given the number of loops to execute.

listing:

```
type
    direction = (up, down, left, right);

procedure ChangeGraphScreen(direction:direction);

var         ByteBuffer :  byte;
offset1, offset2 comp, k,j,i: integer;

begin

if direction in [up,down] then
begin
case direction of
up    :     count:= 7999;   {in this case we work backwards up
                             the screen}
down :      count:= 0;
end;

for i:=0 to 7999 do
for j:=1 to 2 do
begin
offset1:abs(count-i);     {even line followed by odd line}
offset2:=$2000 * (j-1);
ByteBuffer:=GraphScreenBuffer[j,offset1];
GraphScreenBuffer[j,offset1]:=Mem[$B800:i+offset2];
Mem[$B800:offset1+offset2]:=ByteBuffer;
end;
end;
```

```
if direction in [left,right] then
begin
case direction of
left: count:=0;
right:count:=79 {in this case we start with the rightmost
                  columns}
end;

for i:= 0 TO 79 DO
    for j:= 0 to 99 do
        for k:=1 to 2 do
    begin
    offset1:=j * 80 + abs(count-1);
    offset2:=$2000 * (k - 1);
    ByteBuffer:=GraphScreenBuffer[k,offset1];
    GraphScreenBuffer[k,offset1]:=Mem[$B800:offset1+offset2];
    Mem[$B800:offset1+offset2]:=ByteBuffer;
end;
end;

end;
```

declarations: None.

NOTES:

Transfer is slower than in the previous procedures (some 3 seconds for the whole screen).

Note that the screen is loaded continuously without interruption due to the seperation between odd and even lines.

As the unit of transfer is a byte, the screen is filled in four-pixel groups in medium resolution mode and in eight-pixel groups in high resolution mode.

restrictions on use: None.

3.13 Procedure KeepGraphWindow

We shall now apply the techniques we have been developing for the whole screen to the handling of windows. There is, however, a major difference: since Turbo Pascal provides the procedures GetPic and PutPic for transferring screen zones, we can avoid long screen memory address computation procedures.

syntax: KeepGraphWindow;

function:
Stores the contents of the active window in memory.

mechanism:

Simple application of GetPic.

listing:

```
procedure KeepGraphWindow;

begin

SelGraphWindow(ActiveGraphWindow); {precaution in case a
                                    frame is being used}
GetPic(GraphWindowBuffer[ActiveGraphWindow],
0,0,XGraphLimit,YGraphLimit);
end;
```

declarations: None.

NOTES:

This function can also be used to store the background over which a window is opened. This is assumed to have been done when the procedure MoveGraphWindow is used.

restrictions on use: None.

3.14 Procedure ChangeGraphWindow

As in the case of the whole screen, it is useful to be able to load from a window buffer without losing the current contents of the window.

syntax: ChangeGraphWindow;

function:
Exchanging the contents of the active window with the contents of its buffer.

pseudo-code:

a. load the contents of the window into a temporary variable
b. display the contents of the buffer
c. load the buffer with the contents of the temporary variable into the buffer.

mechanism:

GetPic and PutPc make the job considerably easier.

listing:

```
{$ Graph.p}
procedure ChangeGraphWindow;

var
    TempBuffer:OneWindowBuffer;

begin

SelGraphWindow(ActiveGraphWindow); {precaution in case a
                                    frame is being used}
```

```
GetPic(TempBuffer,0,0,XGraphLimit,YGraphLimit);
{saves the active window}

PutPic(GraphWindowBuffer[ActiveGraphWindow],0,YGraphLimit);
{displays the contents of the buffer}

GraphWindowBuffer[ActiveGraphWindow]:=TempBuffer;
{loads the active window into the buffer}

end;
```

declarations: None.

NOTES:

The procedure is rapid to the point that it seems instantaneous. Again, it is clear that judicious declarations can limit the size of code.

restrictions on use: None.

3.15 Procedure MoveGraphWindow

Moving graphics windows, thanks to PutPic and GetPic, is much more rapid than with the case of text windows.

syntax: MoveGraphWindow (deltax, deltay);
deltax and deltay are of the integer type;

function:

Moves the active window by deltax and deltay, carrying out any checks necessary on screen limits.

pseudo-code:

a. check the validity of the movements requested
b. if not valid, correct them
c. exchange the window with its buffer
d. define the new window
e. select it
f. exchange the window and its buffer.

mechanism:

Simple use of the procedures defined previously.

listing:

```
procedure MoveGraphWindow(deltax,deltay:integer);

var
    newx1,newx2,newy1,newy2:  integer;
```

```
begin

{compare the movement requested with the screen}
{or window limits}

    if (GraphWinRefTable[ActiveGraphWindow,1]+deltax < 0)
        then
           deltax:=-GraphWinRefTable[ActiveGraphWindow,1];

    if (GraphWinRefTable[ActiveGraphWindow,2]+deltay < 0)
        then
            deltay:=-GraphWinRefTable[ActiveGraphWindow,2];

    if (GraphWinRefTable[ActiveGraphWindow,3]+deltax
                                             > XModeLimit)
        then
            deltax:=XModeLimit-
                    GraphWinRefTable[ActiveGraphWindow,3];

    if (GraphWinRefTable[ActiveGraphWindow,4]+deltay  200)
        then
            deltay:=200-
                    GraphWinRefTable[ActiveGraphWindow,4];

{correct if too big}

SelGraphWindow(ActiveGraphWindow); {precaution in case frame
                                    used}

ChangeGraphWindow;                 {restores the previous
                                    background}

newx1:=GraphWinRefTable[ActiveGraphWindow,1]+deltax;
newx2:=GraphWinRefTable[ActiveGraphWindow,3]+deltax;
newy1:=GraphWinRefTable[ActiveGraphWindow,2]+deltay;
newy2:=GraphWinRefTable[ActiveGraphWindow,4]+deltay;

DefGraphWindow(ActiveGraphWindow,newx1,newy1,newx2,newy2);

                     {defines and selects }
                     {the new window position}

SelGraphWindow(ActiveGraphWindow);

ChangeGraphWindow;         {saves the new background}

end;
```

declarations: Procedures SelGraphWindow, ChangeGraphWindow, Graph.p (from Turbo Pascal disk).

NOTES:

The original background of the starting position of the window is assumed to have been saved using KeepGraphWindow.

restrictions on use: None.

3.16 Procedure FrameGraphWindow

As for text windows, a frame makes the window easier to see.

syntax: FrameGraphWindow (color);

color is of the byte type.

function:

Draws a frame of colour color around the active window.

pseudo-code:

a. draw the 4 sides of a frame
b. automatically select the window within the frame to save it.

listing:

```
procedure FrameGraphWindow(color:byte);

begin

    Draw(0,0,XGraphLimit,0,color);
    Draw(0,0,0,YGraphLimit,color);
    Draw(XGraphLimit,0,XGraphLimit,YGraphLimit,color);
    Draw(0,YGraphLimit,XGraphLimit,YGraphLimit,color);

    {store the edge: frame}
    GraphWindow(GraphWinRefTable[ActiveGraphWindow,1]+1,
                GraphWinRefTable[ActiveGraphWindow,2]+1,
                GraphWinRefTable[ActiveGraphWindow,3]-1,
                GraphWinRefTable[ActiveGraphWindow,4]-1);

end;
```

declarations: None.

NOTES:

As for text windows, the effect of storing the frame can be overridden by:

SelGraphWindow
KeepGraphWindow
ChangeGraphWindow
MoveGraphWindow.

If required, the frame will have to be protected by calling FrameGraphWindow or declaring the protection process seperately, as we did in the text mode, though this seems less necessary here.

restrictions on use: None.

3.17 Procedure DefPattern

The following procedures make it possible to use procedures Pattern and FillPattern more easily, by defining a library of patterns referenced by their number.

syntax: DefPattern (number, byte1,byte2,byte3,byte4,byte5,
byte6,byte7,byte8);

all parameters are of the byte type.

function:
Uses a number to reference the eight bytes necessary to define a pattern.

listing:

```
procedure DefPattern(number, byte1,
                             byte2,
                             byte3,
                             byte4,
                             byte5,
                             byte6,
                             byte7,
                             byte8: byte);

var
    buffer:patt;

begin

    buffer[0]:=byte1;
    buffer[1]:=byte2;
    buffer[2]:=byte3;
    buffer[3]:=byte4;
    buffer[4]:=byte5;
    buffer[5]:=byte6;
    buffer[6]:=byte7;
    buffer[7]:=byte8;

    PatternLib[number]:=buffer

end;
```

declarations: None.

NOTES: None.

restrictions on use: None.

3.18 Procedure SelPattern

This process is identical to that of selecting a world or a window.

syntax: SelPattern (number);

number is of the byte type.

function:

(i) Activates the pattern specified by number.
(ii) Updates the number of the active pattern.

listing:

{$I Graph.p}

```
procedure SelPattern(number:byte);

begin
    if number in[1..nbpatterns] then
    begin
    Pattern(PatternLib[number]);
    ActivePattern:=number;
    end;
end;
```

declarations: Extended Graphics.

NOTES: None.

3.19 Procedure FillWindowPattern

This procedure saves you having to work out the coordinates of the zone to fill if you are applying procedure FillPattern to a window.

syntax: FillWindowPattern (color);

color is of the byte type.

function:

Fills the active window with the active pattern in colour color, respecting the edges defined (and any frame, if present).

listing:

{$I Graph.p}

```
procedure FillWindowPattern(color:byte);

begin
    SelGraphWindow(ActiveGraphWindow); {precaution in case
                                         of frame;}
```

```
    FillPattern(1,1,XGraphLimit-1,YGraphLimit-1,color);
end;
```

declarations: Extended Graphics.

NOTES: None.

restrictions on use: None.

3.20 Procedures for saving screens and windows to disk

The following procedures are simply implementations of procedures Bsave and Bload, which we shall study later, applied to screens and windows.

syntax: SaveGraphScreen (userfile);
LoadGraphScreen (userfile);
SaveGraphWindow (userfile);
LoadGraphWindow (userfile);

userfile is of the type filespec = string [40].

function:

Saving or loading a screen or window image using the file specified.

NB: The transfer takes place from or to the specified screen or window buffer. This means that the display will be unchanged until the buffer handling procedures described above are used. So SaveGraphScreen does not save the currently displayed screen, but the screen saved in GraphScreenBuffer.

The same applies to windows.

listing:

```
{for these procedures, see explanations}
{of BSave and BLoad}

procedure SaveGraphScreen (userfile:filespec);

begin
Bsave(Seg(GraphScreenBuffer),Ofs(GraphScreenBuffer),
16000, userfile);
end;

procedure LoadGraphScreen (userfile:filespec);

begin
Bload(Seg(GraphScreenBuffer),Ofs(GraphScreenBuffer), 16000,
userfile);
end;

procedure SaveGraphWindow(userfile:filespec);
```

```
begin
Bsave(Seg(GraphWindowBuffer[ActiveGraphWindow]),

Ofs(GraphWindowBuffer[ActiveGraphWindow]),
graphwindowsize, userfile);
end;

procedure LoadGraphWindow(userfile:filespec);

begin
Bload(Seg(GraphWindowBuffer[ActiveGraphWindow]),

Ofs(GraphWindowBuffer[ActiveGraphWindow]),
graphwindowsize, userfile);
end;
```

declarations: Procedures Bsave and Bload.

NOTES:

The reader is referred to the chapter on miscellaneous procedures and functions for detailed information about these procedures.

Note, however, that saving a screen image only affects the code colour and the actual colour depends on the active palette. As no header is saved at the start of the file, restoration of the image will depend on the graphic mode active at the moment of loading. It is up to the user to deal with this problem.

restrictions on use: None.

CHAPTER 5

Joystick

1 ESSENTIAL INFORMATION

For certain readers, the possibility of installing a joystick on an IBM PC will be of little interest. However, the procedures described here can, with a little modification, be adapted to peripherals of the same type and using the same board. The following procedures are therefore, in a sense, of educational value. Moreover, a joystick can be used for many other things besides games, and we leave it to the reader's imagination to find new applications for it.

Turbo Pascal has no standard joystick management procedures. Joystick management is a very specific operation which depends closely on the hardware used. We shall see that it is, however, relatively easy to define such procedures if a reasonable methodical approach is adopted. All that is needed is to have some information on the way this peripheral works.

First of all, your system must have the analogue board called the Game Control Adapter. This board is relatively cheap and its equivalent is included in certain multi-function boards available from retail outlets.

Port 201H:

This port makes it possible to check at any moment what the joystick's state is, i.e. to find out the coordinates of the handle and the state of the push buttons (pressed or released). The port can handle two joysticks and, even though this is not a particularly useful facility, we shall take it into account as we write our procedures.

Here is the structure of port 201H:

—bit 7 set to 0 : button D pressed
—bit 6 set to 0 : button C pressed
—bit 5 set to 0 : button B pressed
—bit 4 set to 0 : button A pressed
—bit 3 set to 1 : stick B—Y-axis—Single shot active
—bit 2 set to 1 : stick B—X-axis—Single shot active
—bit 1 set to 1 : stick A—Y-axis—Single shot active
—bit 0 set to 1 : stick A—X-axis—Single shot active.

The meaning of bits 4 to 7 is easy to see, the same is not true of bits 0 to 3. What is a single shot?

What happens is that whatever data are sent to port 201H, bits 0 to 3 are automatically set to value 1. They remain at this value for a certain time, proportional to the resistance in the corresponding circuit within the joystick. The value of that resistance is a direct function of the position of the joystick in the axis in question. The resistance is 0 on both axes when the joystick is in the upper left position and maximal when it is in the bottom right position. In other words, for joystick A, for example, bits 0 to 1 will almost immediately fall to 0 after port 201H has been addressed if the joystick is in the upper left position, but will remain set to 1 for a certain time if the joystick is in the bottom right-hand position. Obviously, the time involved, which depends on the hardware, will have to be taken into account in calibration.

Knowing these elementary facts allows us to build up a complete set of joystick management functions without difficulty and without using the assembler. This is made possible by the rapidity of Turbo Pascal.

2 AIMS OF THIS CHAPTER

As for graphics procedure, this chapter is a set of interdependent procedures and functions forming a consistent whole. We shall study the following procedures and functions in turn:

GameAdapter	—returns true if the game adapter is connected
Trigger	—returns true if the button has been pressed
JoystickCal1	—calibration of the 0 point on the potentiometer
JoystickCal2	—calibration of 100% point on the potentiometer
XCoordinate	—X-coordinate of the joystick automatically translated into the coordinate system of the current mode, whether text or graphics
YCoordinate	—the same for y
StickDir	—returns a mnemonic code representing the current inclination of the joystick (N, S, E, W, NW, NE, SW, SE).

Caution:

Any changes made to the algorithm for calculating the timer duration will necessarily have consequences for the various functions. In any case, the algorithm must remain common to all the functions and execute in a fixed sequence if the calibration calculations are to remain valid.

The calibration procedures are only called once in the program, unless the video mode is changed.

The accuracy of the result of X and YCorodinate functions depends on the quality of potentionmeters used in the joystick. In any case, we recommend that the absolute values of the co-ordinates should only be used if it is absolutely necessary. The function StickDir will be generally more reliable and should be sufficient in most cases.

3 PROCEDURES AND FUNCTIONS

Note:

It would take too long to insert a joystick presence test systematically into each call to Xcoordinate and Ycoordinate. It is therefore up to the user to make this test at the beginning of every program. Any call to procedures while the specified joystick is not connected 'hangs' the system with no hope of recovery.

3.1 Function GameAdapter

If your application is to offer a choice between commands entered through the keyboard and through the joystick it must be able to recognize whether the necessary board has been installed and if the joysticks are connected. This is the task of the function below and the one following it.

syntax: GameAdapter;

the value returned is of the boolean type.

function:

Returns true if the Game Control Adapter is installed and false otherwise.

pseudo-code:

a. call interrupt 11H
b. return bit 12 from AX.

mechanism:

Interrupt 11H sends the system configuration to AX using the following code:

—bits 14 and 15	: number of printers
—bit 13	: reserved
—bit 12	: game control adapter installed if = 1
—bits 9 to 11	: number of RS232C boards
—bit 8	: reserve
—bits 6 and 7	: number of drives (00 = 1, 01 = 2, etc.)
—bits 4 and 5	: initial display mode
—bits 2 and 3	: memory volume on the main board
—bit 1	: reserve
—bit 0	: IPL from the floppy disk.

listing:

```
function GameAdapter:boolean;

type

    result = record
              AX,BX,CX,DX,BP,SI,DI,DS,ES,flags:integer;
             end;

var

    params:result;

begin

with params do
begin
intr ($11, params);        {'configuration' interrupt}
GameAdapter:= ((AX and $1000) = $1000); {test bit 12 of AX;}
end;

end;
```

declarations: None.

NOTES:

The information returned by interrupt 11H is relatively limited, which is why we only use it for the joystick.

restrictions on use: None.

3.2 Function JoystickOn

This function is complementary to the preceding one.

syntax: JoystickOn;

the value returned is of the byte type.

function:

Returns 0 if no joystick is connected or valid
1 if joystick 1 is connected
2 if joystick 2 is connected
3 if both joysticks are connected.

pseudo-code:

a. initialize port 201H
b. if after 50 milliseconds bits 0 and 1 are set to 0, position the monitor for joystick 1
c. reinitialize the port
d. as b for bits 2 and 3
e. interpret the value of the monitors.

mechanism:

This function is based on the fact that the single-shot bits of the corresponding joystick will only be reset to 0 if it is actually connected. Otherwise the value obtained is random.

listing:

```
function JoystickOn:byte;

var

    buffer: integer;

begin

    Port[$201]:=Port[$201];   {initialize the single-shot}
    delay (50);
    if (Port[$201] and $03 = 0)    then buffer:=1;
                                   {test after 50 ms}

    Port[$s01]:=Port[$201];
```

```
    delay (50);
    if (Port[$201] and $0C = 0)
        then
        if buffer = 1 then buffer:=3
                      else buffer:=2

         else
         if not (buffer = 1) then buffer:= 0

         JoystickOn:=buffer;
end;
```

declarations: None.

NOTES:

The 50 millisecond delay was determined empirically and may be different for other types of hardware. The value allows for a significant margin of safety.

restrictions on use: None.

3.3 Function Trigger

The easiest problem to solve is that of monitoring the joystick buttons. We simply have to test the value of the bits in question at the right moment.

syntax: Trigger (button);

the value returned is of the boolean type.

function:

Returns true if the button specified by button is pressed at the moment the call is made. Button can take the values a, b, c or d.

pseudo-code:

a. set the delay
b. test the bit corresponding to the specified button.

listing:

```
type trigger_button = (a,b,c,d);

function Trigger(button:trigger_button):boolean;

const sensitivity = 50;

begin
```

```
    delay (sensitivity);
    case button of
    a:   Trigger:=not(Port[$201] and $10 = $10);
    b:   Trigger:=not(Port[$201] and $20 = $20);
    c:   Trigger:=not(Port[$201] and $40 = $40);
    d:   Trigger:=not(Port[$201] and $80 = $80);
    end;
end;
```

declarations: None.

NOTES:

Recommendation: If function trigger is used within a loop the value of constant 'sensitivity' should be reduced if greater sensitivity is required, but increased in proportion to the number of instructions in the loop.

The value proposed avoids repetition of the loop if buttons are pressed briefly.

restrictions on use: None.

3.4 Function GetDelay

This procedure is not designed to be called by the user but provides a basis for all the other important procedures in the chapter. This is why it is declared separately.

syntax: GetDelay (axis, Joystick);

axis is of the byte type,
joystick is of the type handle = (J1, J2).
The value returned is of the integer type.

function:

Returns a value proportional to the time taken to deactivate the single shot corresponding to the joystick and axis specified.

pseudo-code:

a. depending on the joystick selected...
b. initialize port 201H
c. increment two counters (one for each axis)
d. until the two corresponding bits are set to 0
e. assign the value of the counter for the specified axis to the function.

mechanism:

This is a simple loop counter.

listing:

```
type
    handle = (J1, J2);
```

```
var
    XCenterFactor,YCenterFactor,TextFactor  :    byte;
                  XCalibRatio,YCalibRatio  :    real;
                            xlimit,ylimit  :    integer;

function GetDelay(axis:byte;joystick:handle):integer;

var  counterx,countery:integer;

begin
    counterx:=0;countery:=0;
    case joystick of
    J1: begin
       Port[$201]:=Port[$201]; {single shot initialization}
                               {counts down relaxation time}
        repeat
        if (Port[$201] and $01 = $01) then
                               counterx:=Succ(counterx);
        if (Port[$201] and $02 = $02) then
                               countery:=Succ(countery);
        until (Port[$201] and $03 = 0);
        end;

    J2: begin
        Port[$201]:=Port[$201];
        repeat
        if (Port[$201] and $04 = $04) then
                              counterx:=Succ(counterx);
        if (Port[$201] and $08 = $08) then
                              countery:=Succ(countery);
        until (Port[$201] and $0C = 0);
        end;
    end;
    case axis of
    1: GetDelay:=counterx;
    2: GetDelay:=countery;
    end;
end;
```

declarations: None.

NOTES:

Changes to the counter calculation algorithms may lead to anomalies.

restrictions on use: None.

3.5 Calibration procedures JoystickCal1 and JoystickCal2

Before using procedures to calculate joystick coordinates the joystick must be calibrated. This is a standard procedure in games programming.

Calibration procedures must be provided for by the applications program before any call to the other functions XCoordinate, YCoordinate and StickDir.

JoystickCal1 assumes that when the procedure is called the joystick is in the top left position.

JoystickCal2 assumes that when the procedure is called the joystick is in the bottom right position.

syntax: JoystickCal1 (joystick);

joystick is of the handle type.

function:

Calculates the eccentricity factor of the coordinates due to the fact that, in the top left-hand position, relaxation times of single shots are never exactly zero.

pseudo-code:

a. count the relaxation time of the bits corresponding to the specified joystick
b. assign this value to two variables (one per axis).

mechanism:

In top left position the value obtained should, in theory, be zero as the potentiometer resistance is zero in this position. This is, in fact, never the case and the difference must be known and taken into account in subsequent calculations.

listing:

```
procedure JoystickCal1(joystick:handle);
begin
    XCenterFactor:=      GetDelay(1,joystick);
    YCenterFactor:=      GetDelay(2,joystick);
end;
```

declarations: None.

NOTES:

The joystick *must* be in top left position when the procedure is called.

restrictions on use: None.

syntax: JoystickCal2 (joystick);

function:

Calculates all the correction parameters necessary to adjust coordinates to the current display mode automatically. This automatic adjustment makes it possible, for example, to limit coordinates to 1..80 along x and 1..25 along y in 80 column mode.

pseudo-code:

a. test the display mode
b. determine the screen limits as a function of the mode

c. calculate the relaxation time of the bits for the specified joystick, along each axis
d. deduce the eccentricity factor from the values obtained
e. calculate the correction factor to apply to the values returned by counters to adapt them to the current display mode
f. determine if 1 has to be added to the joystick coordinates (origin 1,1 in text mode).

mechanism:

This makes simple use of a rule of three.

listing:

```
procedure JoystickCal2 (joystick:handle);

begin

    TextFactor:=0;
    GetVideo;

    case display_mode of
    0..3 :    begin xlimit:=colnum;    ylimit:=25;
                                         TextFactor:=1; end;
    4..5 :    begin xlimit:=319;       ylimit:=199;      end;
    6    :    begin xlimit:=639;       ylimit:=199;      end;
    7    :    begin xlimit:=colnum;    ylimit:=25;
                                         TextFactor:=1; end;
end;

  XCalibRatio:=xlimit/ (GetDelay(1,joystick)-XCenterFactor);
  YCalibRatio:=ylimit/ (GetDelay(2,joystick)-YCenterFactor);
  {calculates the ratio between real coordinates and measured
  values}

end;
```

declarations: None.

NOTES:

The joystick *must* be in the bottom right position when the procedure is called.

Example calculation:

Assuming that XcenterFactor and YcenterFactor are both equal to 3. The values found for the counters in bottom right position are respectively 250 and 200. If the current display mode is, for example, 80-column text mode, the calibration factor will be:

—for x: 80/ (250 – 3)
—for y: 25/ (200 – 3)

restrictions on use: None.

3.6 Functions XCoordinate and YCoordinate

We now have all the tools necessary to calculate the joystick coordinates. Remember, however, the recommendations made above; it is better to work on the direction of inclination of the joystick than on absolute values of coordinates.

syntax: XCoordinate or YCoordinate (joystick);

joystick is of the joystick type,
the value returned is of the integer type.

function:

Returns the absolute value of the x- or y-coordinate of the joystick for the current display mode.

pseudo-code:

a. measure the relaxation time of the bits corresponding to the specified joystick
b. deduce the value of the eccentricity factor
c. multiply the result by the correction factor
d. add the text factor (1 or 0)
e. if the value calculated exceeds the screen limits reduce it to the screen limit.

listing:

```
function XCoordinate (joystick:joystick):integer;

var xcor:integer;

begin

xcor:=Trunc((GetDelay(1,joystick)-XCenterFactor)
          * XCalibRatio) + TextFactor;

case display_mode of
0..3 :    if xcor < 1 then xcor := 1;
4..6 :    if xcor < 0 then xcor := 0;
   7 :    if xcor < 1 then xcor := 1;
end;

if xcor  xlimit then xcor := xlimit;
Xcoordinate:=xcor;

end;

function YCoordinate(joystick:joystick):integer;

var ycor:integer;

begin

ycor:=Trunc ((GetDelay(2,joystick)-YCenterFactor)
              * YCalibRatio) + TextFactor;
```

```
case display_mode of
0..3 :     begin
           if ycor > 25  then ycor:= 25;
           if ycor < 1   then ycor:= 1;
           end;
4..6 :     begin
           if ycor > 200 then ycor:= 200;
           if ycor < 0   then ycor:= 0;
           end;
  7  :     begin
           if ycor > 25  then ycor:= 25;
           if ycor < 1   then ycor:= 1;
           end;
end;

Ycoordinate:=ycor;

end;
```

declarations: None.

NOTES: None.

restrictions on use: None.

3.7 Function StickDir

This function uses the joystick coordinate calculations above to determine in which direction it is leaning. For a games program, for example, it is usually the direction in which an object must move that matters rather than its actual position.

syntax: StickDir (joystick);

the value returned is of the string[2] type.

function:

Returns a mnemonic code made up of one or two characters representing the direction in which the specified joystick is leaning.

Codes are as follows:

up	NW	N	NE
	W	C	E
down	SW	S	SE
	left		right

pseudo-code:

a. divide the screen into nine equal sectors
b. call XCoordinate and YCoordinate
c. find out the sector in which the point corresponding to these coordinates falls.

mechanism:

This simple mechanism is easy to understand, it is based on the no less simple functions already considered above.

listing:

```
type zone = string[2];

function StickDir (joystick:handle):zone;

var  xcor, ycor, right_limit, left_limit,
                 top_limit, bottom_limit      :integer;

procedure wherestick;    {location on the basis of
coordinates}
begin
    if    (xcor <= right_limit)     and
          (xcor >= left_limit)      and
          (ycor <  upper_limit)
                                         then StickDir:='N'
    else
    if    (xcor <= right_limit)     and
          (xcor >= left_limit)      and
          (ycor >  lower_limit)
                                         then StickDir:='S'
    else
    if    (xcor <  left_limit)      and
          (ycor >= upper_limit)     and
          (ycor <= lower_limit)
                                         then StickDir:='W'
    else
    if    (xcor >  right_limit)     and
          (ycor >= upper_limit)     and
          (ycor <= lower_limit)
                                         then StickDir:='E'
    else
    if    (xcor >  right_limit)     and
          (ycor <  upper_limit)
                                         then StickDir:='NE'
    else
    if    (xcor <  left_limit)      and
          (ycor >  left_limit)
                                         then StickDir:='NW'
    else
    if    (xcor >  upper_limit)     and
          (ycor <  lower_limit)
                                         then StickDir:='SE'
    else
    if    (xcor <  left_limit)      and
          (ycor >  lower_limit)
```

```
                                        then StickDir:='SW'
    else StickDir:='C';

    end;

begin                              {determination of coordinates}
    xcor:=XCoordinate(joystick);
    ycor:=YCoordinate(joystick);
    right_limit:=xlimit-(xlimit div 3);{zone limits along x}
    left_limit:=xlimit div 3;

    {definition of y limit}
    case display_mode of
    0..3:       begin upper_limit:=8;  lower_limit:=16;  end;

    7:          begin upper_limit:=8;  lower_limit:=16;  end;

    4..6:       begin upper_limit:=66; lower_limit:=132;  end;

end;

Wherestick;  {return the code}

end;
```

declarations: None.

NOTES:

The zone limits occur at intervals of one third of the screen along x and y.

restrictions on use: None.

CHAPTER 6

Keyboard

1 ESSENTIAL INFORMATION

We shall not here be considering the operation of the IBM PC keyboard in any detail. We shall simply review the information we need the most in order to examine the implementation of certain operations in more detail.

1.1 The keyboard buffer

If you have been using your PC for some time already you will undoubtedly have noticed that you can 'type ahead', allowing you to enter commands without waiting for the operation currently under way to complete. The Intel 8048 microprocessor can remember up to 20 key strokes but the BIOS routines handling the keyboard only provide for a 15-character buffer zone. (Note that this provision is only available in Turbo Pascal if you compile your programs with the C-switch.)

This buffer zone is at address 41EH but we shall not need to access it directly. The state of the buffer is, however, important when it comes to receiving special characters called extended code characters. We shall return to this subject later.

To manage this buffer there are two pointers at addresses 41AH and 41CH which point at the beginning and end of the buffer respectively, and vary as a function of the number of characters waiting. When the two pointers are equal, there are no characters waiting.

1.2 The state zone

At addresses 417H and 418H there are two bytes representing the state of the most important keys on the board, the so called toggle keys, i.e. keys which lead to a change from one mode to another or back again each time they are pressed (Ins, NumLock, ScrollLock, etc...). In detail these two bytes are as follows:

address 417H:

—bit 7 set to 1 : Insert active
—bit 6 set to 1 : Caps Lock on
—bit 5 set to 1 : NumLock on
—bit 4 set to 1 : ScrollLock on
—bit 3 set to 1 : Alt + Shift active
—bit 2 set to 1 : Ctrl + Shift active
—bit 1 set to 1 : LeftShift on
—bit 0 set to 1 : RightShift on.

address 418H:

—bit 7 set to 1 : Insert pressed
—bit 6 set to 1 : Caps Lock key pressed

—bit 5 set to 1 : NumLock key pressed
—bit 4 set to 1 : Scroll Lock key pressed.

The other bits are unused or of no interest.

The most important byte is naturally the first, since knowing whether the insert key has been pressed or not at a given moment is only important if you know whether or not insert is active once we have stopped pressing the key. The information provided by byte 418H allows us to test within a loop whether or not one of the keys mentioned is currently being pressed or not. In what follows we shall not refer again to this address, but only to byte 417H.

There are two ways of accessing information on the state of keys.

The value of byte 417H can be read directly, but this is not good practice as it is not certain that the corresponding information will always be at this address in the future.

It is better to use interrupt 16H of the BIOS, function 2, which will always know where to find the data required. This is the method we shall use here.

On the other hand, in order to force the state zone, we shall have to write directly to the address in question.

1.3 Extended codes

All the characters available on the IBM PC are represented by a code which can take values between 0 and 255. To represent special keys, such as function keys, we use a so-called extended code based on an integer in which the least significant byte is 0 and the most significant byte represents the extended code.

Unlike BASIC, which returns codes based on the convention above, Turbo Pascal returns extended codes in the form of an escape sequence followed by the code for the extended character. If therefore we are trapping for an escape character in a keyboard read process, we have to test whether another character is waiting to be read and then process it as an extended code. We shall use the following two ways of implementing such decoding.

1.4 Interrupts

We shall use two interrupts to manage the keyboard.

1 Interrupt 16H on the BIOS which covers three functions
2. DOS function 0CH.

There are others but we shall not make use of them.

2 AIMS OF THE CHAPTER

Procedure Read applied to file Kbd and function KeyPressed are particularly useful. However, you will sometimes need to know or force the state of the keyboard to make your applications friendlier to their users.

Furthermore, the detection of special keys will always be a difficult task for anybody who cannot immediately remember the value of the corresponding codes. We shall propose some simple procedures providing solutions to these problems. Thanks to them we shall be able to:

—obtain the status of the keyboard	—KbdStat
—force the position of the toggle keys	—SetKbd
—initialize the keyboard	—ResetKbd
—flush the keyboard buffer	—ClearKbd
—read in a waiting character	—Inkey
—discover what character is waiting before reading the buffer	—WaitingChar

The reader should also consult the chapter on input/output and procedures InputString, InputReal and InputInt which give a good illustration of what can be done in the way of replacing standard procedures (if they are not appropriate for some reason or another) based on a clear understanding of how the keyboard and screen work.

3 PROCEDURES AND FUNCTIONS

Apart from a common declaration for function KbdStat and procedure SetKbd (type keytype), these two procedures, as well as procedures ResetKbd and ClearKbd are independent of each other.

Functions XlateExt and XlateSimple can only be used internally by procedure Inkey and function WaitingChar.

3.1 Function KbdStat

Programs with any sophistication at the input/output level will often need to determine the state of keys on the keyboard. Given the information listed above, this will pose no problem.

syntax: KbdStat (key);

key is of the keytype type = (ins, caps, numlock, scrollock, altshift, ctrlshift, leftshift, rightshift);

the value returned is of boolean type.

function:

Returns true if the key corresponding to the specified type is active.

E.g.: KbdStat(ins) is true if the Insert key is active.

pseudo-code:

a. load function number 2 into AH
b. call interrupt 16H of the BIOS (keyboard)
c. prepare the mask corresponding to the specified key
d. compare this mask with the information in AL.

mechanism:

Function 2 of interrupt 16H returns the status of keyboard keys in AL in the same way as we would find them in address 417H (see above).

listing:

```
type
    keytype =   (ins,caps,numlock,scrollock,altshift,
                ctrlshift,leftshift,rightshift);
    {will also be used later}

function KbdStat (key:keytype):boolean;

type
    result = record
              AX,BX,CX,DX,BP,SI,DI,DS,ES,flags:integer;
             end;

var
    params:   result;
bit_buffer :   byte;

begin
params.AX:=$200;
intr($16,params);

case key of
ins         :   bit_buffer:=$80;   {determination of the}
caps        :   bit_buffer:=$40;   {comparison of the mask for}
numlock     :   bit_buffer:=$20;   {AL}
scrollock   :   bit_buffer:=$10;
altshift    :   bit_buffer:=$08;
ctrlshift   :   bit_buffer:=$04;
leftshift   :   bit_buffer:=$02;
rightshift:     bit_buffer:=$01;
end;

KbdStat:=(Lo(params.AX) and bit_buffer) = bit_buffer;

end;
```

declarations: None.

NOTES: None.

restrictions on use: None.

3.2 Procedure SetKbd

To make your programs friendlier for the user, you can force the state of keys on the keyboard before, for example, proceeding to data entry. This could be useful in editing too. With this procedure you can force entry in capitals or initialize the numeric keypad when numeric data is to be entered.

syntax: SetKbd (key, state);

key is of the keytype type,
state is of the status type = (on, off).

function:

Forces the state of the key specified in the same way as if it were actually being pressed.

pseudo-code:

a. prepare the mask corresponding to the specified key for each of the two states
b. if the state = on, set the bit to 1
c. if the state = off, set the bit to 0.

mechanism:

No comments to make. The same as KbdStat (but with the opposite effect).

listing:

```
type
    status = (on, off);
    Keytype = (ins,caps,numlock,scrollock,altshift,
              ctrlshift,leftshift,rightshift);

procedure SetKbd(key:keytype;state:status);

var
    bit_buffer : byte;

begin
case state of

on:
begin
    case key of
    ins         :  bit_buffer:=$80;  {prepares a mask with}
    caps        :  bit_buffer:=$40;  {a bit set to 1}
    numlock     :  bit_buffer:=$20;  {in the position for the}
    scrollock   :  bit_buffer:=$10;  {key specified}
    altshift    :  bit_buffer:=$08;
    ctrlshift   :  bit_buffer:=$04;
    leftshift   :  bit_buffer:=$02;
    rightshift:    bit_buffer:=$01;
    end;
    Mem[0:$417]:=Mem[0:$417] or bit_buffer;
    end;

off:
    begin
    case key of
```

```
    ins        :  bit_buffer:=$7F;     {as above but set to 0}
    caps       :  bit_buffer:=$BF;
    numlock    :  bit_buffer:=$DF;
    scrollock  :  bit_buffer:=$EF;
    altshift   :  bit_buffer:=$F7;
    ctrlshift  :  bit_buffer:=$FB;
    leftshift  :  bit_buffer:=$FD;
    rightshift:   bit_buffer:=$FE;
    end;
    Mem[0:$417]:=Mem[0:$417] and bit_buffer;
    end;
end;

end;
```

declarations: None.

NOTES:

Here we have access to byte 417H directly as there is no BIOS function available to carry out this operation by way of an interrupt.

restrictions on use: None.

3.3 Procedure ClearKbd

It is sometimes necessary to test the keyboard, to carry out 'housekeeping' so as not to process parasite information as a result of accidental pressing of keys. Note, however, that keystrokes are not buffered in Turbo Pascal unless compilation switch C is set to –.

syntax: ClearKbd;

function:

Clears the keyboard buffer and deletes any waiting character.

pseudo-code:

a loads function number 12 into AH
b. calls DOS interrupt 21H.

mechanism:

Simple interrupt call.

listing:

```
procedure ClearKbd;

type
    result = record
              AX,BX,CX,DX,BP,SI,DI,DS,ES,flags:integer;
             end;
```

```
var
    params: result;

begin
    params.AX:=$0c00;     {DOS function 12 but without}
                          {an associated function call}
    MsDos (params);
    end;
```

declarations: None.

NOTES:

It is PC DOS function 12 which clears the keyboard. We also have to bear in mind that this function normally accompanies keyboard clearing with the execution of one of the following functions whose number is loaded in AL:

function 1	:	keyboard entry. Character held in AL
function 6	:	console I/0
function 7	:	character entry with no screen echo
function 8	:	the same with interrupt monitoring
function A	:	buffered entry.

We only mention these details out of interest as they will not be of any major value to us here. In this operation we therefore leave AL set to 0.

restrictions on use: None.

3.4 Procedure ResetKbd

If we want to start an entry operation through the keyboard with all keys at the non-active state, this short procedure is all we need to call.

syntax: ResetKbd;

function:
Sets all toggle keys on the keyboard to off.

mechanism:
Sets byte 417H to 0.

listing:

```
procedure ResetKbd;

begin memw[0:$417]:=0; end;
```

3.5 Procedure Inkey and function WaitingChar

The reader may wonder why it is useful to set up a procedure for reading characters typed at the keyboard when the standard procedure Read applied to the standard file Kbd will do the job perfectly well. This is an entirely valid objection when we are dealing with normal ASCII characters, but the same is not true if we are trying to detect either function keys, or special combinations such as ALT + character or CONTROL + character.

Though the Turbo Pascal and Turbo Tutor manuals provide ways of detecting an extended code, they do not give (and this is not their aim) any means of interpreting them simply.

The procedures we are proposing will allow you to recognize, by use of a simple mnemonic code, whether a particular function key has been pressed or whether a particular combination of keys has been transmitted.

3.5.1 Internal procedures XlateExt and XlateSimple

We first of all need a tool to translate keycodes which transforms them into an easily storable character string. These functions are of no interest from a technical point of view as they simply transform a byte into a four-character string. We therefore include no comments other than the listing itself.

We shall simply examine the mechanism used in XlateExt, to translate Alt + character combinations, a mechanism which makes use of the role of constants. The constant keyboard is an image of the American keyboard which remains the standard for key search codes.

XlateSimple translates the character code into a mnemonic string in cases where the code is not an extended code. XlateExt does the same for extended code. These functions have to be declared before Inkey and WaitingChar.

listing:

```
type  readkey = string[4];

function XlateSimple(code:byte):readkey;

begin
if not(code in [7,8,9,10,13,27])  then
XlateSimple:=char(code);
XlateSimple:=char(code);
case code of
08   :   XlateSimple:='BSP'; {if a useful special
                              character...}
09   :   XlateSimple:='TAB'; {conversion into a mnemonic
                              string}
13   :   XlateSimple:='ENT'; {BSP for backspace}
27   :   XlateSimple:='ESC'; {TAB for the tab key}
end;                          {ENT for enter}
end;                          {ESC for escape}

function XlateExt(code:byte):readkey;

{Detailed explanations of these mnemonic codes}
{are given with our description of Inkey.}
{All these codes are in the BASIC documentation for your PC}
```

```
const
    keyboard : string[26] = 'QWERTYUIOPASDFGHJKLZXCVBNM';

var symbol_code : string[2];
    keybuffer   : readkey;

begin
case code of

15    :     keybuffer:='STAB';

16..25 : keybuffer:='A-'+keyboard[code-15]; {Alt + character}
30..38 : keybuffer:='A-'+keyboard[code-19]; {combination}
44..50 : keybuffer:='A-'+keyboard[code-24];

59..68 : begin
           Str (code-58:2,symbol_code);        {PF keys}
           keybuffer:='F'+symbol_code;
           if not (code = 68) then keybuffer [2]:='0';
    end;

71    :     keybuffer:='HOME';
72    :     keybuffer:='CSUP';
73    :     keybuffer:='PGUP';
75    :     keybuffer:='CSLF';
77    :     keybuffer:='CSRG';
79    :     keybuffer:='END';
80    :     keybuffer:='CSDN';
81    :     keybuffer:='PGDN';
82    :     keybuffer:='INS';
83    :     keybuffer:='DEL';
84..113    :    begin
    Str((code-83) mod 10:2, symbol_code);
    if (code in [93,103,113]) then symbol_code:='10';
    case code of
    84..93    :keybuffer:='SF' + symbol_code; {Shift + PF
keys}
    94..103   :keybuffer:='CF' + symbol_code; {Ctrl + PF
keys}
    104..113  :keybuffer:='AF' + symbol_code; {Alt + PF keys}
    end;
    if not (code in [93,103,113]) then keybuffer[3]:='0';
    end;

114  : keybuffer:='FSCR'; 115 :keybuffer:='CCSL';
116  : keybuffer:='CCSR'; 117 :keybuffer:='CEND';
118  : keybuffer:='CPGD'; 119 :keybuffer:='CHOM';

120..128 : begin
             Str(code-119:2,symbol_code);
```

```
            keybuffer:='A' +symbol_code[2];   {Alt + figure}
          end;

129   : keybuffer:='A-0';
132   : keybuffer:='CPGU';

end; {of case}

XlateExt:=keybuffer;

end;
```

3.5.2 Procedure Inkey

Inkey makes use of the functions we have just been considering to meet the aim we set ourselves of returning the meaning of keys in decoded form.

syntax: Inkey (keycode);

keycode is of the readkey type = string [4];
note that keycode is passed by reference.

function:

Returns, in keycode, a symbolic representation of the character waiting at the keyboard if it is an extended code character or the character itself if it is a normal character.

Only the most common extended ASCII characters have a symbolic representation. If needed, other symbols can be added.

The procedure only returns control to the program once a character has actually been read. A call to procedure Inkey therefore leaves the system waiting for a character and returns the character or its symbolic representation. If no representation has been provided the code returned is 'ERR'.

As mnemonic codes are easier to remember, we now have an easy way of examining the keyboard in order to detect most characters without having to concern ourselves with the corresponding codes.

mnemonics:

BSP	: backspace	TAB	: tab key	ENT	: enter
ESC	: escape	HOME	: home	PGUP	: page up
PGDN	: page down	END	: end	DEL	: delete
INS	: insert	PSCR	: control print screen	CSUP	: up arrow
CSDN	: down arrow	CSLF	: left arrow	CSRG	: right arrow
CEND	: control end	CHOM	: control home	CPGU	: control page up
CPGD	: control page down	CCSL	: control left arrow	CCSR	: control right arrow

Fnn : Pf key from 01 to 10 alone
SFnn : Pf key from 01 to 10 + shift
CFnn : Pf key from 01 to 10 + control
AFnn : Pf key from 01 to 10 + alternate
—i.e. 40 possibilities for function keys
A–x : alternate + character
A–n : alternate + figure

pseudo-code:

a. read the keyboard character
b. if the character is not Escape and keypressed is false (no second character waiting) we are dealing with a simple ASCII character: call XlateSimple
c. otherwise we are dealing with an extended character code: call XlateExt.

mechanism:

Remember the comments made above about the way Turbo Pascal returns extended codes: an escape character and a second character (extended code).

So if the first character is escape, and there is another following it, we are dealing with an extended code character.

listing:

```
procedure Inkey(var keycode:readkey);

{KEYCODE must be of the string [4] type}

var  ch:char;

begin
    keycode:='ERR.';
    read(kbd,ch);
if not((ch=#27) and keypressed)     {not'ERR.';
read(kbd,ch);
if not((ch=#27) and keypressed)     {not an extended code}
then
    keycode:=XlateSimple (ord(ch))
else                                {an extended code}
    begin
    read(kbd,ch);
    keycode:=XlateExt(ord(ch));
    end;
end;
```

declarations: XlateSimple and XlateExt.

NOTES:

We have now implemented character reading 'in the style of' Turbo Pascal.

We could have used interrupt 16H, function 0. The character read would then have been in AL.

An important comment needs to be made on this question.

If the program using Inkey was compiled with the C switch set to –, which has to be the case if you want to use the following function (WaitingChar), the following may occur:

Since touching the F1 function key, for example, is recognized by Turbo Pascal as an escape sequence followed by ; (semi-colon, ASCII character 59), if you press Escape followed by a semi-colon, Inkey will recognize the sequence as a depression of Key F1. The same is true for all the other extended code keys.

The only way of avoiding this is to use interrupt 16H to read the character in exactly the same way as WaitingChar (below) but using function 0 (read the character) instead of function 1 (test the waiting character).

This is not a major disadvantage in most cases but it does need to be pointed out, since the fact is not covered in the Turbo Pascal documentation.

restrictions on use: None.

3.5.3 Function WaitingChar

This function behaves in a similar way to Inkey but with one fundamental difference. The character waiting is tested but not read. This allows us to decide in advance what it is we have to do.

Let us look at this in detail.

syntax: WaitingChar;

the value returned is of the readkey type.

function:

Returns the mnemonic code of the waiting character but without reading it, which means that the character is still waiting in the keyboard buffer. *This only works if the C compilation switch is set to '–'.*

This allows all sorts of tests to be carried out and a decision to be made on what to do with the waiting character before it has even left the buffer.

The standard boolean function Keypressed shows whether or not a character is waiting in the buffer. If no representation is provided for the code, the string returned is 'ERR'. If no character is waiting, the string returned is empty.

pseudo-code:

a. load function number 1 into AH
b. call interrupt 16H
c. test bit 6 of flags (zero flag)
   if bit 6 = 0 a character is waiting, then
   c1. if AL <> 0, ordinary character: XlateSimple
   c2. if AL = 0, extended code character then

c21. read extended character in AH
c22. call XlateExt

d. if bit 6 = 1 then no character waiting, return an empty string.

mechanism:

Function 1 of interrupt 16H operates as follows:

If there is a character waiting, the zero flag (ZF) of the indicator register is set to 0.

If the character waiting is an extended code character, AL is set to 0 and the code is in AH. Otherwise the code for the simple ASCII character will be in AL.

listing:

```
function WaitingChar:readkey;

var
    params    :    result;
    read_code :    byte;

begin
    WaitingChar:='';
    with params do
    begin
    AX:=$100;
    intr($16, params);
    if (params.flags and $40) = 0 then {test if ZF=0 (zero
                                                    flag)}
    begin          {equivalent to keypressed}
    Waitingchar:='ERR.';
    if not (Lo(AX)=0) then begin        {simple ASCII code}
                   read_code:=Lo(AX);
                   WaitingChar:=XlateSimple(read_code);
            end
            else begin                 {extended code}
                 read_code;=Hi(AX);
                 WaitingChar:=XlateExt(read_code);
            end;
    end;{of flags test}
    end;{of with params do}
end;
```

declarations: XlateSimple and XlateExt.

NOTES:

At the end of the procedure the character is still waiting in the keyboard buffer and will remain there until read (kbd,ch), Inkey or ClearKbd are used.

ZF is the zero flag of the 8088 indicator register and it is that flag, in this BIOS interrupt, which shows whether or not a character is waiting.

To work, this procedure *must* be compiled with the {$C –} switch. This switch concerns the whole of a program block and cannot be redefined. It is often worth setting it to –, as leaving it active slows execution of the program.

restrictions on use: None.

CHAPTER 7

Floppy disks

1 ESSENTIAL INFORMATION

There is so much information available on floppy disks that it could easily fill several chapters on its own. It is not our aim to go over the ground already covered by others, but only to give information and reminders indispensable to the reader to understand the procedures and functions we shall consider in this chapter.

1.1 Simple ideas on disk organization

The information stored in the form of bytes on a disk is held in individual basic units called sectors (i.e. a sector is the minimum amount of information that has to be handled to provide access to a particular data item). Sectors are in turn organized into tracks.

For PC-DOS, sectors contain 512 bytes and there are 40 tracks on the disk. These values are invariable unless specific modifications are made to the BIOS (special formatting functions).

What may vary with the different DOS versions is the configuration of the system, i.e. the number of sectors per track, which can be 8 or 9, and the number of sides to the disk. Disk sides are numbered 0 and 1. Sectors are numbered starting from 1. Tracks are numbered from 0 to 39.

Every disk must include a sector called the *boot record* which is used to initialize the system. It is always on side 0 and in sector 1 of track 0.

Following the boot record, there is a file allocation table (FAT) which handles allocation of sectors to files. This allocation takes place sector by sector for single sided disks and by groups of 2 sectors for double sided disks.

These allocation units are called *clusters*. The FAT always exists in two copies, for security reasons.

The following sectors contain the directory, and the number of sectors allocated to it depends on the format of the disk. Here is the detailed structure of that allocation, which is rarely given in documentation:

—single side/ 8 sectors.

FAT : side 0 sectors 2 and 3
DIR : side 0 sectors 4 to 7

—single side/ 9 sectors.

FAT : side 0 sectors 2 to 5
DIR : side 0 sectors 6 to 9

—double sided/ 8 sectors.

FAT : side 0 sectors 2 and 3
DIR : side 0 sectors 4 to 8
side 1 sectors 1 to 2

—double sided/ 9 sectors.

FAT : side 0 sectors 2 to 5
DIR : side 0 sectors 6 to 9
side 1 sectors 1 to 3.

Detailed information about the contents of these sectors is given in any good book on the IBM PC and DOS systems. For our purposes we need only save the following:

The first byte of the FAT always contains a code representing the disk type:

—FF double sided disk / 8 sectors per track
—FE single sided disk / 8 sectors per track
—FD double sided disk / 9 sectors per track
—FC single sided disk / 9 sectors per track.

The sequence FF7 in FAT sector (which is organized in groups of 12 bits) indicates a defective sector.

In the directory, each file is represented by a group of 32 bytes whose structure is as follows:

—bytes 0 to 7	:	file name
1st byte	=	00 : location has never been used
		E5 : deleted file
—bytes 8 to 10	:	extension
—byte 11	:	attribute 00H : normal, 01H : read only,
		02H : hidden, 04H : system
		08H : the first 11 bytes are the disk label
		10H : sub-directory
		20H : archiving bit
—bytes 12 to 21	:	reserved
—bytes 22 to 2	:	time of last update
—bytes 24 to 25	:	date of last update
—bytes 26 to 27	:	number of first cluster in file (the others will be provided by the FAT)
— bytes 28 to 31	:	size of file in bytes.

Note that, as in many information systems, data using more than one byte are stored with the least significant byte first.

1.2 Basic ideas on disk data transfer

Any writing or reading of data to or from a disk has to go through a buffer called the DTA (Data Transfer Area). By default, the DTA is at offset 80H of the PSP (Program Segement Prefix). The PSP is a zone allocated by DOS at the start of execution of a program. COM precedes it. Its length is 256 bytes and it contains all data necessary for communication between DOS and the program. Function CSeg always refers to the start of the PSP and the real code starts at offset 100H.

Since this default DTA is 128 bytes long, reading an entire sector will have to take place elsewhere. We shall see how to define an address for the DTA ourselves. Fortunately, for all classic operations, Turbo Pascal carries out the task for us transparently.

We need to be fully aware of the fact that we cannot read less than one sector on a disk, even if we only need a few bytes of information. Buffers of sufficient size will always have to be provided if direct reading or writing of disk data is to take place.

1.3 Interrupts

For direct reading or writing of sectors, we shall use BIOS interrupt 13H. For file handling, we shall have to use DOS services, but we shall do nothing in this area as Turbo Pascal already handles the necessary services in a very complete way.

Interrupt 13H provides six services for floppy disks. They allow us to read or write one or more sectors, and to check the result of these operations.

Certain DOS functions, on the other hand, allow us to handle the DTA and to build up certain simple utilities.

NB:

Readers familiar with DOS and its interrupts will perhaps wonder why we do not make use of interrupts 25H and 26H for reading or writing sectors. It is true that these two interrupts are easier to use than interrupt 13H. Unfortunately, the two interrupts use a particular way of passing return parameters making them completely incompatible with procedure Intr (this is a specific characteristic of the stock handling methods used).

To make use of them, we would have to use assembly language. That would take us outside the aims of this book.

2 AIMS OF THE CHAPTER

It is always infuriating to see a program 'hang' simply because a drive door is open or because attempts to write protected disks were not detected. These little problems are not generally taken into account by high level languages. We want to help you solve them using the following procedures, whose guiding themes will be:

—reading / writing sectors
—checking return codes
—default drive (selection and determination)
—space available on disk
—number of defective clusters
—determination of the disk type
—handling of the DTA
—reading the directory.

We shall not consider operations on files here as Turbo Pascal is very flexible in this field and it is difficult to see how we could improve on it.

3 PROCEDURES AND FUNCTIONS

The procedures and functions that follow were written on the assumption that the system used had two drives. If an extension box has been fitted to allow for other drives, minor modifications are necessary. These routines do not apply to a hard disk.

3.1 Procedures ReadSector and WriteSector

These procedures are the basic tools for disk management and make it possible to read or write to disk without going through the concept of a file. It is naturally necessary to be very careful in using these procedures and to take care that no important data are deleted. The information given above concerning reading information in the FAT or directory should be borne in mind when these procedures are used. We have used them ourselves to produce a data protection program establishing a password for access to data on disk.

syntax: ReadSector (nbsec, trk, sec, side, dev, segment, offset);
WriteSector (nbsec, trk, sec, side, dev, segment, offset);

all parameters are of the integer type.

function:

Read or write were more sectors on the disk using the following parameters:

—nbsec = number of sectors read or written (0..8)
—trk = track number (0 to 39)
—sec = sector number (1 to 9)
—side = disk side (0 or 1)
—dev = drive number (a = 0, b = 1)
—segment = address of the buffer segment to receive data or
to provide data for writing.
—offset = offset of this buffer.

Segment and offset are generally provided by the standard functions Seg and Ofs.

The global variables WriteOk and ReadOk are updated with the return code for the operation, which has the following meaning:

0 : operation successful
1 : unknown command
2 : address zone not found
3 : writing to a write-protected disk
4 : sector not found
8 : DMA capacity exceeded
9 : data transfer crossing page limit (64k)
16 : invalid date
32 : controller error
64 : incorrect positioning on a track (difficulty with arm)
128 : time out (the controller did not reply in time).

The latter code is the most useful as it is the code returned if the drive is empty or the drive door was not properly closed.

This provides us with a first means of obtaining the return code for the operation. We shall propose another later to obtain the return code for an input/output operation on disk carried out by a standard procedure.

These codes supplement those provided by the standard function IOresult.

pseudo-code:

a. load function number 2 or 3 into AH and the number of sectors into AL
b. load the track number into CH and the sector number into CL
c. load the disk side into DH and the drive number into DL
d. load the buffer segment into ES and the offset into BX
e. call the disk interrupt
f. if the CARRY FLAG (first bit of the indicator register) is set to 0: the operation was successful else...
   f1.obtain the error code from AH and load it into variables WriteOk and ReadOk.
   f2.reinitialize the controller calling DOS function 13
g. loop until the operation succeeds or the number of the attempt is equal to 5 (or 3 for writing).

mechanism:

We shall use two interrupts here:

—interrupt $13 for the operation as such
—DOS function 13 to reinitialize in case of failure.

Unlike the DOS functions, which take a certain number of precautions in file handling, no checking is carried out on the drive motor rotation speed before reading starts. Errors are therefore possible at the first attempt. If this occurs, we have to reset and start again. If five attempts are not enough, there really is a major problem.

listings:

```
var ReadOk:byte;

procedure ReadSector
(nbsec,trk,sec,side,dev,segment,offset:integer);

type
    result = record
                AX,BX,CX,DX,BP,SI,DI,DS,ES,flags:integer;
             end;

var
    params    :    result;
    index     :    integer;

begin
    index     :=0;
    repeat
    params.AX:=$0200 or nbsec;
    params.CX:=trk shl 8 or sec;
```

```
params.DX:=side shl 8 or dev;
params.ES:=segment;
params.BX:=offset;

index:=index+1;      {count the number of attempts}
intr($13, params);

if not(odd(params.flags)) then ReadOk:=0
                          else ReadOk:=Hi(params.AX);

{if bit 0 of flags (CF) is set to 0 : operation
 successful;}
{else AH contains the error code}

if not (ReadOK=0)    then
                     begin
                     params.AX:=$0D00; {reset controller}
                     MsDos (params);
                     end;

until (ReadOk=0) or (index=5); {stop when OK or after 5
                                    attempts}
end;

var WriteOk:byte;

procedure WriteSector (nbsec,trk,sec,side,dev,segment,
                         offset:integer);

type
    result = record
              AX,BX,CX,DX,BP,SI,DI,DS,ES,flags:integer;
             end;

var
    params     :    result;
    index      :    integer;

begin     {same mechanism as ReadSector}
index:=0;
repeat
params.AX:=$0300 or nbsec;
params.CX:=trk shl 8 or sec;
params.DX:=side shl 8 or dev;
params.ES:=segment;params.BX:=offset;

index:=index+1;
intr($13,params);

if not (odd(params.flags)) then WriteOK:=0 else
        WriteOk:=Hi(params.AX);
```

```
    if not (WriteOk=0)  then
                        begin
                        params.AX:=$0D00;
                        MsDos(params);
                        end;
    until (WriteOk=0) or (index=3);

end;
```

declarations: None.

NOTES: Careful!!

restrictions on use: Does not apply to the hard disk.

3.2 Function OpStatus

If you do not want to use global variables to obtain the return code, this function will provide you with the same service using local variables. Note that it only works after basic operations of the ReadSector or WriteSector type.

syntax: OpStatus;

the value returned is of the byte type.

function:

Returns the error code of the last input/output operation carried out on the disk. The meaning of the codes is shown above.

pseudo-code:

a. load function number 1 into AX
b. call the disk interrupt
c. return the code.

mechanism:

Simple interrupt call.

listing:

```
function OpStatus:byte;

type
    result = record
              AX,BX,CX,DX,BP,SI,DI,DS,ES,flags:integer;
             end;

var

params:  result;
```

```
begin
    params.AX:=$0100;        {same mechanism as read and write}
                             {but without reading or writing}
    intr ($13,params);

if not (odd(params.flags)) then OpStatus:=0
                              else OpStatus:=Hi(params.AX);
end;
```

declarations: None.

NOTES: Same comment on the role of flags as above.

restrictions on use: Does not apply to the hard disk.

3.3 Procedure VerifySwitch

For all disk write operations, DOS provides the possibility of checking the data transferred. This is the same option as in the /v parameter of the DOS command COPY. Here we show how it can be applied.

syntax: VerifySwitch (choice);

choice is of the switch type = (on,off).

(Careful to avoid duplicate declaration with the status type in the chapter on the keyboard.)

function:

Activates or deactivates the DOS verify switch.

pseudo-code:

a. load function number $2E into AH; if choice = on, AL: = 1, else AL: = 0
b. set DL to 0
c. call the DOS interrupt.

mechanism:

Simple DOS call
DL must be set to 0.

listing:

```
type switch = (on,off);

procedure VerifySwitch(choice:switch);

type
    result = record
               AX,BX,CX,DX,BP,SI,DI,DS,ES,flags:integer;
             end;
```

```
var
    params : result;
begin
 if choice=on then params.AX:=$2E01 else params.AX:=$2E00;

 {bit 0 of AX set to 1 or to 0}
 {call function}

 params.DS:=params.DS and $FF00;    {DL must be zero}
 MsDos(params);
 end;
```

declarations: None.

NOTES:

The verification procedure takes time and therefore slows down disk write operations considerably.

restrictions on use: None.

3.4 Procedures SetDta and GetDta

As we saw before, the data transfer zone from and to the disk can be defined by the user. If Turbo Pascal is left to manage the DTA, we may sometimes need to know where it is or where to set an address for it. These DOS facilities will allow you to do so.

Note, however, that the segment and offset of the data transfer buffer for a file are also accessible using the FIB (File Interface Block) managed by Turbo Pascal and on which detailed information is provided in the manual. The segment and offset of the FIB are accessible by applying functions Seg and Offset to variable filvar representing the file.

Procedure GetDta

syntax: GetDta (segment, offset);

segment and offset are of integer type and are passed by reference.

function:

Returns the segment and offset of the DTA in segment and offset.

pseudo-code:

a. load function number 47 into AH
b. call the DOS interrupt
c. read segment in ES and offset in BX.

mechanism:

Simple call to DOS.

listing:

```
procedure GetDta(var segment,offset:integer);
```

```
type
    result = record
              AX,BX,CX,DX,BP,SI,DI,DS,ES,flags:integer;
             end;

var
    params: result;

begin
    params.AX:=$2F00;          {function $2F}
    MsDos(params);

    segment:=params.ES; {read segment and offset}
    offset:=params.BX;
    end;
```

declarations: None.

NOTES: None.

restrictions on use: None.

Procedure SetDta

syntax: SetDta (segment,offset);

segment and offset are of the integer type.

function:

Positions the DTA at address segment : offset.

pseudo-code:

a. load function no 26 into AH
b. load offset and segment into DS and DX
c. call DOS.

mechanism:

Simple DOS call.

listing:

```
procedure SetDta(segment,offset:integer);

type
    result = record
              AX,BX,CX,DX,BP,SI,DI,DS,ES,flags:integer;
             end;

var
    params:result;
```

```
begin
    params.AX:=$1A00;     {function $1A}
    params.DS:=segment; {passing segment}
    params.DX:=offset;  {passing offset}

    MsDos(params);
    end;
```

declarations: None.

NOTES: None.

restrictions on use: None, but be careful...

3.5 Disk management procedures and functions

If you do not want to have to return to DOS to find out how much space is available on a disk, if you want to change the default drive from inside your programs, if you want to know the number of effective buffers on a diskette and if, finally, you want to know from within the programs what format the diskette is, your wishes will soon be met.

NB:

The disk type = (a,b) is declared once for all these functions.

3.5.1 Function DiskType

syntax: DiskType (d);

d is of the disk type. The value returned is of the byte type.

function:

Returns a code representing the format of the disk:

1: double sided : 8 sectors per track
2: single sided : 8 sectors per track
3: double sided : 9 sectors per track
4: single sided : 9 sectors per track.

pseudo-code:

a. read the first sector of the FAT of the specified disk
b. test the first byte of the sector
c. return the corresponding code.

mechanism:

Use of ReadSector.
See above for the meaning of the first byte of the FAT.

listing:

```
type disk = (a,b);
```

```
function DiskType(d:disk):byte;

var
    drive     :    byte;
    buffer    :    array[0..511] of byte;

begin

    drive:=ord(d);

ReadSector(1,0,2,0,drive,Seg(buffer),Ofs(buffer));
{read the first sector of the FAT}

case Buffer [0] of        {disk type in first byte}
$FF  :    Disktype:=1;
$FE  :    Disktype:=2;
$FD  :    Disktype:=3;
$FC  :    Disktype:=4;
end;

end;
```

declarations: ReadSector.

NOTES: None.

restrictions on use: None (floppy disks).

3.5.2 Function DefDrive

syntax: DefDrive;
the value returned is of the char type.

function:
Returns a character representing the default drive (a,b,...)

pseudo-code:
a. load function number 25 into AH
b. call the DOS interrupt
c. read the drive code in AL.

mechanism:
The code returned is 0, 1, etc.... You simply have to add 97 (the ASCII code for a) to convert it into a character.

listing:

```
function DefDrive:disk;

type
```

```
    result = record
               AX,BX,CX,DX,BP,SI,DI,DS,ES,flags:integer;
             end;

var
    params:result;

begin
    params.AX:=$1900;
    MsDos(params);
    DefDrive:=disk(Lo(params.AX));        {i.e. if AL = 0}
                                          {use of Retyping}
end;
```

declarations: None.

NOTES: The character returned is in lower case.

restrictions on use: None.

3.5.3 Procedure SetDrive (in version 3.0 of Turbo Pascal use ChDir)

syntax: SetDrive (d);

d is of the disk type.

function:

Selects the default drive depending on the value of d (a,b).

pseudo-code:

a. load function number 14 into AH
b. load the drive number into DH (0 for a, 1 for b, etc.)
c. call DOS.

mechanism:

Note simply that ord (d) takes values 0 if d = a, 1 if d = b, etc.

listing:

```
procedure SetDrive(d:disk);

type
    result = record
               AX,BX,CX,DX,BP,SI,DI,DS,ES,flags:integer;
             end;

var
    params:result;

begin
    params.AX:=$E00;       {function $E}
```

```
    params.DX:=ord(d);     {passing drive number}
    MsDos(params);
end;
```

declarations: None.

NOTES:

Note that, on return from the procedure, AL contains the total number of drives in the system if there are more than two, and two otherwise!

restrictions on use: None.

3.5.4 Function DiskSpace

syntax: DiskSpace (d);

d is of the disk type. The value returned is of the real type.

function:

Returns the amount of free space left on the specified disk, in kilobytes.

pseudo-code:

a. load function number 54 into AH
b. load the drive number (different convention) into DH
c. call the DOS
d. if AX = FFFFH the drive is invalid—return 0
e. space = AX ∗ BX ∗ CX /1024.

mechanism:

On return from the interrupt, the contents of the registers are as follows:

AX contains the number of sectors per cluster
BX contains the number of clusters available
CX contains the number of bytes per sector.

Care must be taken not to multiply the three parameters directly, in order to avoid an overflow error.

listing:

```
function DiskSpace(d:disk):real;

var
 params:result;
 Space:real;
     n:byte;

begin
    n:=ord(d)+1;          {different convention for this
                           function}
```

```
    params.AX:=$3600;     {n = 0 is the default drive}
    params.DX:=n;         {in this case write
                           DiskSpace(DefDrive)}
    MsDos(params);

    if params.AX=$FFFF then Space:=0;  {drive not valid}
    Space:=params.AX * params.BX; {two-stage calculation to
                                   avoid overflow}
    Space:=Space * params.CX / 1024;

    DiskSpace:=Space;

end;
```

declarations: None.

NOTES: None.

restrictions on use: None.

3.5.5 Function DiskOK

syntax: DiskOk (d);

d is of the disk type. The value returned is of the byte type.

function:

Returns the number of bad clusters recorded in the FAT. These are unusable clusters marked FF7H.

pseudo-code:

a. read the two sectors following the boot record on the specified disk
b. determine the disk type
c. for the 512 or 1024 bytes read, check the presence of an FF7 sequence in a position compatible with the 12 bits period of FAT information (see above)
d. count each occurrence of this sequence.

mechanism:

The difficulty is that we can only process bytes, even though information in the FAT uses 12 bits.

We therefore have to look for FFH or F7H sequences at valid positions and check whether the four bits that follow or precede it are equal to 7H or FH.

listing:

```
function DiskOk(d:disk):integer;

var
    drive,base,offset,
```

```
    counter,index,i      : integer;
            buffer       : array [0..1023] of byte;

begin
    drive:=ord(d);
    base:=Seg(Buffer);offset:=Ofs(buffer);
    ReadSector (2,0,2,0,drive,base,offset);
    if (Mem[base:offset]=$FD) or (mem[base:offset]=$FC)  then

index:=2
    {FAT covers one or two sectors depending on format} else

index:=1;
    counter:=0;

    for i:=0 to 512*index-1 do

    begin

    if (Mem[base:offset+i]=$FF) and ((i mod 6=0)
                                or (i mod 6=3)) then

    if ((Mem[base:offset+i+1]) and $F0 = $70)
                         then counter:=Succ(counter);
    {if a byte is equal to $FF and its ordinal number is a}
    {multiple of 3 or 6, check whether the following digit
     is 7}

    if (Mem[base:offset+i]=$F7) and ((i mod 6=2)
                               or (i mod 6=5)) then

    if ((Mem[base:offset+i-1]) and $F = $F)
                              then counter:=Succ(counter);
    {if a byte is equal to $F7 and its ordinal number is a}
    {multiple of 2 or 5, check whether the preceding digit
     is F}

    end;

DiskOk:=counter

end;
```

declarations: None.

NOTES:

If there are two useful sectors for the FAT, there is no break in data for the two sectors. The last four bits of the first sector and the eight first bits of the second sector form a valid piece of information on a cluster number.

restrictions on use: None.

3.6 Functions FirstEntry and NextEntry

Most applications require handling of files and therefore directories. The following two functions will allow you to find the name of the files contained in a particular directory, corresponding to a search mask as well as a file attribute.

3.6.1 Function FirstEntry

syntax: FirstEntry (path, attribute);

path is of the pathname type = string [63]. Attribute is of the integer type. The value returned is of TYPE entry = string [12].

function:

Returns the name of the first file whose name corresponds to the specified path.
The path is in fact a mask which uses DOS conventions:

—the character string may contain the name of the drive, the name of the directory and the name of the file
—the name of the file may be a complete name or a mask using the wild characters * and ?, as in DOS commands.

The attribute is that specified for the DOS file, i.e.:

—bit 0 set to 1 : read-only file
—bit 1 set to 1 : protected file (not listed in the DIR)
—bit 2 set to 1 : system file
—bit 3 set to 1 : no file: disk label
—bit 4 set to 1 : sub-directory
—bit 5 set to 1 : correctly closed file present.

examples:

FirstEntry ('????????.com',$20) returns the name of the first non-protected file whose extension is .COM and which is on the default drive.

FirstEntry ('a: ???????? .com', $22) does the same thing but on drive a and includes protected files.

If no file corresponding to the specified mask exists, the string returned is 'No Such File'.

pseudo-code:

a. initialize variables
b. save the current Dta and install the new one
c. obtain the mask from a character ARRAY
d. load function number $4E into AX
e. load the specified attribute into CX
f. load the mask address into DS and DX
g. if error, obtain the code
h. else obtain the name of the file character by character
i. return the Dta to its original state.

mechanism:

The Dta has to be initialized to a variable capable of receiving information returned by the system. Such information is coded over a length of 43 bytes as follows:

—bytes 1 to 21 : reserved for DOS
—byte 22 : attribute found
—bytes 23 and 24 : time file was written
—bytes 25 and 26 : date file was written
—bytes 27 to 30 : size of file
—bytes 31 to 43 : name and extension of file (12 characters including the stop plus a 0 as delimiter).

After a call to DOS function $4E, the Dta contains all this information. All we have to do is to obtain it, using an extremely simple procedure whereby each character in the Dta is written to the buffer assigned to receive the filename, starting from offset 29.

listing:

```
type
    entry     = string[12];
    pathname  = string[63];
    path_mask = array [1..63] of char;

var
    mask : path_mask;                  {file search mask}
    Dta  : array [1..43] of byte; {data zone}
                              {common variable for both
                               functions}

function FirstEntry(path:pathname;option:integer):entry;

var
        params                      :    result;
        entry_buffer                :    entry;
    saved_segment,saved_offset,i    :    integer; {to return
                                                    the system}
                                         {to its initial state}

begin
    Fillchar(Dta,SizeOf(Dta),0);         {initialize variables}
    Fillchar(Mask,SizeOf(Mask),0);
    Fillchar(entry_buffer,SizeOf(entry_buffer),0);

    GetDta(saved_segment,saved_offset);{save the Dta}
    SetDta(Seg(Dta),Ofs(Dta));           {install the new Dta}

    for i:=1 to Length(path) do mask[i]:=path[i];
                                         {obtain the mask}
    params.AX:=$4E00;           {function 'find first'}
    params.CX:=option;          {attribute byte in CX}
```

```
    params.DS:=Seg(mask);      {point on mask}
    params.DX:=Ofs(mask);
    MsDos(params);

    if odd(params.flags)       {error : Carry Flag set to 1}
    then
        case Lo (params.AX) of
        2 : FirstEntry := 'No Such File';   {error in AX}
       18 : FirstEntry := 'No More File';
        end

    else
    begin      {obtains the file name from the Dta}
    i:=1;      {and locates the length of the string}
    repeat
    entry_buffer[i]:=Char(Mem[Seg(Dta):Ofs(Dta)+29+i]);
    i:=Succ(i);
    until not (entry_buffer[i-1] in [' '..'']) or (i > 13);
    entry_buffer[0]:=Char(Pred(i));
    FirstEntry:=entry_buffer;
    end;

    SetDta(saved_segment,saved_offset);{returns the system}
    end;                               {to its initial state}
```

declarations: SetDta and GetDta.

NOTES: None.

restrictions on use: None.

3.6.2 Function NextEntry

syntax: NextEntry (attribute);

attribute is of the integer type. The value returned is of the entry type = string [12].

function:

Returns, after a call to FirstEntry, the name of the next file corresponding to the same specifications. If there are no further files corresponding to the specifications passed, the string returned is 'No More Files'.

mechanism:

Exactly the same as FirstEntry, except that the parameters no longer need to be passed as they are held in the Dta and the function number called is $4F.

listing:

```
function NextEntry(option:integer):entry;
```

```
{behaves in exactly the same way as FirstEntry but it is}
{not necessary to pass parameters: they are still in the}
{Dta, on condition that NextEntry is used after FirstEntry}

var
              params            :    result;
          entry_buffer          :    entry;
saved_segment,saved_offset,i   :    integer;

begin
    Fillchar(entry_buffer,SizeOf(entry_buffer),0);

    GetDta(saved_segment,saved_offset);
    SetDta(Seg(Dta),Ofs(Dta));

    params.AX:=$4F00;
    params.CX:=option;
    MsDos(params);
    if odd (params.flags) and (Lo(params.AX) = 18)
        then
            NextEntry := 'No More Files'
        else
            if not (odd(params.flags))
            then
            begin
            i:=1;
            repeat
entry_buffer[i]:=Char(Mem[Seg(Dta):Ofs(Dta)+29+i]);
              i:=Succ(i);
              until not(entry_buffer[i-1] in [' ' .. '~'])
                                                  or  (i>13);
              entry_buffer[0]:=Char(Pred(i));
              NextEntry:=entry_buffer;
              end;

        SetDta(saved_segment,saved_offset);
        end;
```

declarations: SetDta and GetDta.

NOTES:

This routine cannot function if a call to FirstEntry has not been made first.

A call to FirstEntry followed by repeated calls to NextEntry will scan the whole or part of the directory for files corresponding to the specifications passed.

restrictions on use: None.

CHAPTER 8

Printer

1 ESSENTIAL INFORMATION

A relatively small amount of information is necessary about the printer. We shall simply discuss the printer status byte and the command character sequences that can be sent to the printer.

1.1 Status byte

The three functions of interrupt 17H (despatch of a character to the printer (0), initialization of the printer port (1) and reading of its status (2)) return the printer status byte in AH. Here is its structure.

—bit 7 : printer available for printing
—bit 6 : reception
—bit 5 : no more paper
—bit 4 : printer selected
—bit 3 : input/output error
—bit 2 : unused
—bit 1 : unused
—bit 0 : time out.

The meanings in the list above assume that the relevant bit is set to 1. For the printer to print a character, bits 7 and 4 must be set, and therefore AH must have a value 90H.

1.2 Command characters

Command characters make the printer carry out special actions such as a form feed or a switch into a particular printer mode (double strike, single direction, etc.).

For the standard IBM printer, there are eight print modes apart from the graphics mode. Not all these modes can be combined with each other. One of the following has to be chosen:

—normal mode
—condensed mode (132 characters a line)
—bold character modes

and then one of:

—double strike mode
—subscripting
—superscripting

and then:

—double width
—underline.

Transmission of a printer command is generally announced by sending an escape character followed by one or several further characters. We shall not go into detail on these codes which appear in the PC USER GUIDE.

2 AIMS OF THIS CHAPTER

In this chapter, we shall apply three utilities allowing us to:

—check the state of the printer before attempting to print
—include command character sequences in mnemonic form within a byte instruction
—set or change tab positions.

It is easier to use mnemonic codes, rather than always having to remember command codes.

3 PROCEDURES AND FUNCTIONS

3.1 Function PrinterOk

syntax: PrinterOk;

the value returned is of the boolean type.

function:

Returns true if the printer is ready to print.

pseudo-code:

a. load function number 2 into AH
b. load the printer number (from 0 to 4) into DX
c. call interrupt 17H
d. read the status byte from AH and test it.

mechanism:

Simple BIOS call.

listing:

```
function  PrinterOk:boolean;

type

    result = record
               AX,BX,CX,DX,BP,SI,DI,DS,ES,flags:integer;
             end;
```

```
var
    params : result;

begin
    params.AX:=$200;                         {function2}
    params.DX:=0;                            {printer number}
    intr($17,params);
    PrinterOk:=(Hi(params.AX) = $90);        {test bits 7 and 4}
end;
```

declarations: None.

NOTES: None.

restrictions on use: None.

3.2 Procedure ParseCommand

This procedure, which is of general utility, makes it possible to handle a character string or character group separated by the / character. The calling block has to pass the command string by reference, and that string is returned with the first command removed and sent to the specified buffer.

This procedure allows command characters for the printer, in the procedures below, to be properly handled.

syntax: ParseCommand (command,buffer);

command is of the command string type = string [255], buffer is of the command buffer type = string [4]. These parameters are passed by reference.

function:

Truncates 'command' from that part of the string running from the first character up to a / character.

Sends this part of the string to a buffer.

pseudo-code:

a. if no /: single command
b. then buffer = command and command = empty string
c. else buffer = start of string; buffer and / are deleted from command.

listing:

```
type
    commandstring = string[255];
    commandbuffer = string[4];

procedure ParseCommand   (var command:commandstring;
                           var buffer :commandbuffer);
```

```
begin
    if Pos ('/',command)=0    {only one parameter}
    then

begin
    buffer:=Copy(command,1,4);     {read parameter}
    command:='';
end
else
begin
buffer:=Copy(command,1,Pos('/',command)-1);
{paramter=start at string up to}

Delete(command,1,Pos('/',command));
{deletion of parameter read}

end;
end;
```

declarations: None.

NOTES: None.

restrictions on use: None.

3.3 Function SetPrt

Rather than always having to remember more or less obscure codes, it is worth setting up a function which can be used within a write construction and which makes it possible to change printer mode as flexibly as possible or to issue line feeds or form feeds without having to consult PC manuals.

syntax: SetPrt (command);

command is of the commandstring type. The value returned is also of the commandstring type.

function:

Translates a mnemonic code into a string of characters immediately usable by the printer. The conventions are as follows:

HT	:	horizontal tab	ALxx	:	advance by xx lines
Pxx	:	number of lines/page	CR	:	carriage return
AP	:	advance page	CM	:	condensed mode
DM	:	double width mode	BM	:	bold mode
EC	:	end condensed	ED	:	end double width
EB	:	end bold	UM	:	underline mode
DS	:	double strike	OD	:	one-directional printing
EU	:	end underline	ES	:	end double strike

EO	:	end one directional printing	SB	:	subscript
SP	:	superscript	ES	:	end subscript or superscript.

E.g.: Write (lst, SetPrt ('AL5/EM/HT')

executes a five-line advance,
switches into bold mode,
advances to the next tab position.

Spaces and lower case characters are allowed.

pseudo-code:

a. initialize an empty buffer
b. remove spaces
c. while the length of command is non-zero
   c1. call ParseCommand
   c2. convert the buffer to upper case
   c3. determine the printer code and add it to the buffer
d. return the concatenation of all these codes.

mechanism:

All we are doing is translating your commands into the printer codes given in the documentation for your PC.

listing:

```
function SetPrt (command:commandstring):commandstring;

var
    i,lines,result  :    integer;
            buffer  :    string[4];
    func_buffer     :    commandstring;

begin
    func_buffer:='';
    while Pos(' ',command)<>0 do
    delete(command,Pos(' ',command),1);       {delete spaces}

    while not(Length(command))=0 do          {beginning of
                                              conversion}
    begin
    ParseCommand(command,buffer);            {extract a parameter}

    for i:=1 to Length(buffer) do
    buffer[i]:=Upcase(buffer[i]);

    if buffer='HT' {translates each command into a sequence}
                   {usable by the printer and chains the
                    sequences}
```

```
then
func_buffer:=func_buffer+chr(19)    {horizontal tab}
else
if Copy (buffer,1,2)='AL'          {line feed}
then
begin
Delete(buffer,1,2);
Val(buffer,lines,result);
if result=0
then
for i:=1 to lines do
func_buffer:=func_buffer+chr(10);

end
else
if buffer='AP'              {form feed
     then func_buffer:=func_buffer+chr(12)
else
if buffer='CR'              {carriage return}
     then func_buffer:=func_buffer+chr(27)+chr(60)
else
if buffer='CM'              {condensed mode}
     then func_buffer:=func_buffer+chr(15)
else
if buffer='CE'              {end condensed mode}
     then func_buffer:=func_buffer+chr(18)
else
if buffer='DW'              {double width mode}
     then func_buffer:=func_buffer+chr(27)+chr(87)+chr(1)
else
if buffer='ED'              {end double width mode}
     then func_buffer:=func_buffer+chr(27)+chr(87)+chr(0)
else
if buffer='BM'              {bold mode}
     then func_buffer:=func_buffer+chr(27)+chr(69)
else
if buffer='EB'              {end bold mode}
     then func_buffer:=func_buffer+chr(27)+chr(70)
else
if buffer='UM'              {underline mode}
     then func_buffer:=func_buffer+chr(27)+chr(45)+chr(1)
else
if buffer='EU'              {end underline mode}
     then func_buffer:=func_buffer+chr(27)+chr(45)+chr(0)
else
if buffer='DS'              {double strike mode}
     then func_buffer:=func_buffer+chr(27)+chr(71)
else
if buffer='SS'              {end double strike mode}
```

```
        then func_buffer:=func_buffer+chr(27)+chr(72)
    else
    if buffer='SB'             {subscript mode}
        then func_buffer:=func_buffer+chr(27)+chr(83)+chr(1)
    else
    if buffer='SP'             {superscript mode}
        then func_buffer:=func_buffer+chr(27)+chr(83)+chr(1)
    else
    if buffer='ES'             {end subscript or superscript}
        then func_buffer:=func_buffer+chr(27)+chr(84)
    else
    if buffer='OD'             {one-direction printing}
        then func_buffer:=func_buffer+chr(27)+chr(85)+chr(1)
    else
    if buffer='EO'             {end of one-directional
                                printing}
        then func_buffer:=func_buffer+chr(27)+chr(85)+chr(0)
    else
    if Copy(buffer,1,1)='P' {page length}
        then
            begin
            Delete(buffer,1,1); {number of lines}
            Val(buffer,lines,result);
            if ((lines In [1..127])
                and (result = 0))   {valid number}
                then
                func_buffer:=func_buffer+chr(27)
                                        +chr(67)
                                        +chr(lines);
            end;

    end; {end of conversion}

SetPrt:=func_buffer;

end;
```

declarations: ParseCommand.

NOTES: None.

restrictions on use:

If your printer does not accept IBM codes, you will have to make the appropriate modifications to the procedure.

3.4 Procedure SetPrtTab

Printers generally allow logical tab positions to be set. That still leaves it up to you to implement them. This procedure will help you.

syntax: SetPrtTab (tabs);

tabs is of the commandstring type.

function:

Allows you to set n tab positions on the printer. Tabs must contain tab positions in the form of one, two or three digits:

E.g.: SetPrt ('8/9/12/23/34');
will define tab positions 8,9,12,23 and 34.

Spaces are allowed. Values must be less than 132. There cannot be more than 28 tab positions. The print head can be sent to a tab position using command HT in SetPrt.

pseduo-code:

a. remove blanks
b. initialize using Esc D
c. send one tab position after the other (call ParseCommand)
d. end the sequence with chr(0).

listing:

```
procedure SetPrtTab(tabs:commandstring);

var

    result    :    integer;
    buffer    :    string[4];
    position  :    integer;

begin
    while Pos (' '.tabs)<>0 do
    delete (tabs,Pos(' ',tabs),1);        {remove spaces}

    write(lst,chr(27),chr(68));           {mode initialization}

    while not (Length(tabs)=0) do

    begin
    ParseCommand(tabs,buffer);            {reads a position}
    Val(buffer,position,result);

    if (position<133) and (result=0)
    then write(lst,chr(positon));         {if valid,sends it
                                           through}

    end;
```

```
    write(lst,chr(0));                    {end of mode}

end;
```

declarations: ParseCommand.

NOTES: None.

restrictions on use: As for SetPrt.

CHAPTER 9

Input/Output

1 ESSENTIAL INFORMATION

1.1 Data entry

The standard input procedures in Turbo Pascal are covered by rules which may surprise those used to other languages. In particular, editing entries is only possible (and then only in a very restricted way) if the input file is assigned to the console or if the standard input file is used with compilation switch B+. These possibilities for editing are as follows:

—backspace and delete will delete the last character entered.

—Escape and Control X will delete the whole line and send the cursor back to the start of the line.

—Control D recalls a character from the last line entered.

—Control R recalls the last line entered.

Furthermore, assignment of a value to the standard variable BufLen makes it possible to limit input to the number of characters specified. The default value for BufLen is 127, and it returns to the default value after each read operation.

It is therefore impossible to delete a character other than the last one entered or to insert another character in a string that is already entered. If there is an error, the whole string has therefore to be retyped.

The reader will agree that this can be tedious for the user and is perhaps the only major disadvantage of Turbo Pascal.

Our aim in this chapter is to correct this state of affairs.

Before we start, there is some valuable advice we should give readers on the way data entry should be managed using procedures Read and ReadLn. During input of a variable of the integer type, for example, the user inadvertently types a letter in the sequence of figures. If this is not corrected before Enter is pressed, the program will be immediately exited with error 10.

If we want to write programs that are secure at the level of data entry through the keyboard, we shall always have to program them as follows:

the situation is that some variable var has to be read

```
{$I-}
Repeat
Read(var);
IOerror: = IOresult;
IOflag; = (IOerror  0);
if IOflag then
```

```
begin
error handling
end;
until not IOflag;
{$I+}
```

Where IOflag is a boolean variable and IOerror is an integer. This structure should, in our view, be used systematically.

The deactivation of compilation switch I gives the programmer control over operations in the event of input/output errors. All we need, therefore, is to ensure that reading takes place within a loop. After that loop, we test the return code from the operation using the standard function IOresult which must be equal to zero if everything has taken place successfully. Otherwise, an error handlling routine has to be entered which may reposition the cursor at the beginning of the input zone, delete the string displayed and possibly display an error message. The use of IOerror is necessary because IOresult can only be read once before being reset to zero for the next I/O operation.

Procedure InputString which we shall create below overcomes all the disadvantages completely as it allows reading of a string without using procedures Read and ReadLn.

In the same way, we cannot recommend too strongly that users make the greatest possible use of variable Buflen. The best way of avoiding data entry problems is to limit the length of data entry fields.

1.2 Data output

Procedure Write provides fairly complete formatting possibilities as standard. It is possible to define the width of the output field for the data and, when dealing with real values, to set the representation mode and the number of decimal places. However, it is unfortunate that there is no equivalent of BASIC's *print using*. Without going so far as to build up equivalent instructions, we shall see what types of mechanisms can be used to do so.

In the same way, we shall see how we can include tab and space generation functions within a Write instruction.

2 AIMS OF THE CHAPTER

We shall build up all the procedures we need to overcome the difficulties mentioned above, as far as possible. The first, very simple, procedures will provide us with more control over data output, and the data entry procedures suggested will illustrate the use of keyboard management procedures that we studied in the last chapter.

With these procedures as a foundation, you will certainly be able to construct still more efficient routines that are more closely adapted to your applications.

3 PROCEDURES AND FUNCTIONS

3.1 Function StUpcase

This function, covered in the Turbo Pascal manual, is improved here by taking account of the use of accents in certain languages. It is a simple extension of the standard Upcase function.

syntax: StUpcase(str);

str is of the stringmax type = string[255],
the value returned is of the same type.

function:

Returns the input string converted to uppercase.

pseudo-code:

a. for each character in the string...
b. convert the character to upper case
c. if it is an accented character...
d. convert it into the upper case non-accented character.

listing:

```
type stringmax = string[255];

function StUpcase(strin:stringmax):stringmax;

var
    i:integer;

begin
    for i:=1 to Length(strin) do
    begin
    strin[i]:=UpCase(strin[i]);
    if (strin[i] in['é','ê','ë','è']) then strin[i]:='E'
    else
    if (strin[i] in['â','ä','à'])     then strin[i]:='A'
    else
    if (strin[i] in['ï','î',ì])       then strin[i]:='I'
    else
    if (strin[i] in['ü','û',ù'])      then strin[i]:='U'
    else
    if (strin[i] in['ô','ö',ò])       then strin[i]:='O'
    else
    if strin[i] = 'ç'                 then strin[i]:='C';
    end;
    StUpcase:=strin;
end;
```

declarations: None.

NOTES:

The input string does not necessarily have to be of type [255] since it is not passed by reference.

restrictions on use: None.

3.2 Function Spaces

syntax: Spaces(n);

n is of the byte type. The value returned is of the stringmax type.

function:

Returns a string of n spaces.

listing:

```
function Spaces(n:byte):stringmax;

var
    i          : integer;
    buffer     : stringmax;

begin
    buffer:='';
    for i:=1 to n do buffer:=buffer+' ';
    spaces:=buffer;
end;

type linstring = string [80];
```

3.3 Function Tab

To format screens more easily, this function, which can be used with instruction Write, allows the cursor position to be controlled during writing. Its use is equivalent to that of Tab in BASIC.

syntax: Tab(n);

n is of the byte type. The value returned is of the linestring type = string[80].

function:

Generates as many spaces as necessary to put the cursor in column n. If column n precedes the current position of the cursor, positioning takes place in the following line.

E.g.: Write ('here' Tab(40),'... further on');

pseudo-code:

a. test the display mode
b. calculate the number of spaces necessary
c. increase colnum if the position calculated is before the current cursor position.

listing:

```
function Tab(n:byte):linestring;
```

```
var
    Blanks:byte;

begin
    GetScreen;
    if n <= colnum then          {if valid position}
    begin
    Blanks:=n-wherex;            {calculates number of spaces}
    if Blanks < 0  then Blanks:=Blanks+colnum; {move to
                                              following line}
    Tab:=Spaces(Blanks);
    end;
end;
```

declarations: GetScreen.

NOTES:

The function is independent of the display mode.

restrictions on use: None.

3.4 Function IntFormat

The display format for integers in Turbo Pascal allows for little in the way of variation. This relatively simple procedure allows cursor control of display, so that the user can decide whether to show the sign or not and can choose between spaces and zeros to fill gaps in display fields. To fill gaps with spaces, we simply have to use an instruction of the type write (integer:n).

syntax: IntFormat (integer,format);

integer is of the integer type. Format is of the formatstring type = string[6], and so is the value returned.

function:

Converts an integer into a string of characters using the following conventions, specified by format:

\# represents a digit
\+ indicates the sign if it is to be shown
(if the number is negative the sign is always shown).

If the number of digits requested is:

smaller than the number of digits in the number;
the request is overridden to provide the minimum necessary

greater than the number of digits in the number;
the gap is filled with zeros.

This function, included in a write instruction, makes it possible always to have the same number of digits displayed whatever the value of 'integer'.

E.g.: write(IntFormat(n,'+####'));

would give	+0024	if n = 24
	+1234	if n = 1234
	+12345	if n = 12345
	–0034	if n = –34

pseudo-code:

a. function digit (calculates the number of digits in the integer)
   a1. calculate the log base 10 of the integer
   a2. take the integer part (equal to the number of digits – 1)

b. procedure scanformat
   b1. calculate the number of digits requested
   b2. check if the sign has been requested for positive numbers

c. procedure body
   c1. if the number of digits demanded is too small then readjust
   c2. provide as many zeros as there are gaps
   c3. convert the integer to a string
   c4. concatenate the sign, zeros and value buffers.

listing:

```
type formatstring = string[6];

function
IntFormat(nbr:integer;format:formatstring):formatstring;

var
    counter,i :    integer;
    buffer1,
    buffer2 :      formatstring;
    sign      :    string[1];

function digit:integer;

var
    Ln10:real;

    begin
    if not (nbr=0)
    then
    begin
    Ln10:=In(abs(nbr))/Ln(10);      {a little maths!}
    digit:=Trunc(Ln10)+1;           {calculate number of
                                     digits}
```

```
    end
    else
    digit:=1;
    end;

procedure scanformat;

begin
    counter:=0;
    sign:='';
    for i:=1 to Length(format) do
        case format[i] of
        '#' : counter:=Succ(counter); {how many digits?}
        '+' : if nbr >0 then sign:='+';     {sign?}
    end;
end;

begin

scanformat;
if counter <digit then counter:=digit;  {force number of
                                          digits}

buffer1:='';
for i:=1 to counter-digit do buffer1:=buffer1+'0';
                                   {add the missing zeros}

Str(nbr,buffer2);
if nbr <0 then begin
    delete(buffer2,1,1);      {hold the sign in reserve}
    sign:='-';
    end;

IntFormat:=sign+buffer1 + buffer2;

end;
```

declarations: None.

NOTES:

An equivalent procedure can be written for real numbers, though the standard facilities provided are adequate.

restrictions on use: Integers only.

3.5 Procedure InputString

This procedure makes full use of the routines studied in the chapter concerning the keyboard. It is relatively long and we shall attempt to explain it in detail as clearly as possible. The basic principle is to allow capture on screen of a string of characters without using procedure Read, so as to keep full control of string editing. In these conditions, we can avoid the disadvantages mentioned at the start of this chapter.

How can data be entered without using Read or Readln?

The keyboard management procedures that we have established allow a character to be read from the keyboard, as would be done by procedure Read(kbd,ch), but with automatic translation of the code if we are not dealing with a displayable character but with a special character or an extended code character. In this way we could therefore detect the use of the insert, backspace, cursor movement or other such keys, and simply enter the character directly, without using Read. We then have to deal with echoing the character to the screen ourselves, if appropriate.

Readers should, if necessary, revise the chapter about the keyboard.

syntax: InputString(str,attribute);

str is passed by reference and without type. Attribute is of the byte type.

function:

Reads string str, as Read(str) would but allowing extended editing functions.

Attribute defines the appearance of characters in the string during editing. Function Attribute examined in the chapter on the screen could be used to select the colour of the background and of the characters entered without affecting the current values set by TextColor and TextBackGround.

This functionality will be extremely useful to highlight input easily without having to worry about repositioning TextColor and TextBackGround at the end of entry.

Editing Conventions:

—The maximum permitted editing string is 79 characters. However, we do not recommend the use of this procedure for capturing long strings (longer than 40 or 50 characters).

—The maximum length of the string to enter is fixed by the standard variable BufLen which is set to 79 by default. Do not forget to set it to an appropriate value.

—Insert active: insertion of the character typed at the cursor position, shifting of the right-hand side of the string by one position to the right. If the maximum length of the string has been reached, insertion becomes impossible.

—Insert inactive: the character at the current cursor position is overwritten by the new character.

—Backspace: deletion of the character to the left of the cursor; the cursor and the right-hand part of the string move one position to the left.

—Right or left arrow: cursor moves one position to right or left.

—Delete: deletion of the character at the current cursor position and shift of the right-hand side of the string by one position towards the left.

—Home: the cursor moves to the start of the string.

—End: the cursor moves to the end of the string.

—Escape: the whole of the string is deleted and the cursor is moved to the start of the string.

—Enter: end of entry.

Cursor movements to the right generate spaces if the cursor is beyond the end of the string currently being entered.

Note: during editing, the procedure will generate as many spaces on the display as are needed to reach the length specified by size. This allows for deletion of characters using the backspace key.

mechanism:

The length of this procedure prevents our going into details on the mechanism in the way we have generally done for other routines. We shall therefore attempt to explain it in a less formal way.

The basic principle is that characters typed at the keyboard are read, in a loop, after which the system determines whether it is a character to display or a special character causing a particular action to take place. The string to input is held in a buffer (StringBuffer) and the position of the cursor on the screen is managed at the same time as that of a pointer to the corresponding position of the buffer (bufpos).

After each key stroke, the specified modifications are recorded and made effective. The cursor then returns to the starting position for input and the buffer is written again using procedure WriteAttribute to allow control of the character and background colours.

When the enter key is pressed, input is considered to be over and str is assigned the value of StringBuffer.

This assignment takes place using procedure Move, which allows a string variable to be passed without specifying its type. Otherwise we would have had to compile the block with the procedure and positioning switch V set to {$V–}.

The reader would be well advised to take the time to study in depth the way this procedure operates as it will give him a clearer idea of how keyboard management works.

listing:

```
procedure InputString(var str;attribute:byte);

var
                        StringBuffer        :     linestring;
size,x_begin,y_begin,bufpos,xpos,ypos       :     byte;
                                  ch        :     char;
                             keycode        :     string[4];
                                   i        :     integer;

begin
if BufLen >79 then Buflen:=79;  {no input beyond 79
                                 characters}
GetScreen;
x_begin:=WhereX;y_begin:=WhereY;    {start of input position}
```

```
bufpos:=0;
StringBuffer:='';

repeat

size:=Length(StringBuffer);          {what is the length?}
Inkey(keycode);
if (Length(keycode) = 1) and  (Succ(bufpos) <=BufLen)
                         and  (WhereX + 1 <= colnum)

then begin
    ch:=keycode;                        {a normal character}
    if ord(ch) in [32..255] then
    if KbdStat(ins) and (bufpos <= size) and (Succ(size)<=
                                                BufLen)
        then
                       begin
    {insertion}        Insert(ch,StringBuffer,bufpos+1);
                       bufpos:=Succ(bufpos);
                       GoNext;
                       end

                       else if not (KbdStat(ins)) then
                       begin
    {overwrite}        if (size= 0) or (bufpos = size)
                       then StringBuffer:=StringBuffer + ch
                       else StringBuffer [bufpos+1]:=ch;
                       bufpos:=Succ(bufpos);
                       Gonext;
                       end;
    end

    {else special keys}

else
begin
    if (keycode = 'BSP') and (bufpos > 0)
            then begin

    {delete left-hand character}
                    Delete (StringBuffer,bufpos,1);
                    bufpos:=Pred(bufpos);
                    GoPred;
                    end
    else
if (keycode = 'CSRG') and (bufpos <buflen) and (WhereX+1
                                                  <> colnum)
                    then begin
```

```
                                   Gonext;
{one position to the right}        bufpos:=Succ(bufpos);
                                   if bufpos > size then
{+ space if end of string}         StringBuffer:=StringBuffer
                                                       + '';
                                   end

else
if (keycode = 'CSLF') and (bufpos > 0)
            then begin
{one position to the left}         GoPred;
                                   bufpos:=Pred(bufpos);
                                   end

else
{deletion}
if (keycode = 'DEL') and (bufpos+1 in [1..size])
        then Delete(stringBuffer,bufpos+1,1)

else
{start position}
if keycode = 'HOME' then begin
                              GotoXY (x_begin,y_begin);
                              bufpos:=0;
                              end

else
{end of string}
if keycode = 'end' then while not (bufpos=size)
                                   and not (WhereX = colnum)
                                   and not (WhereX = x_begin
                                                + Buflen) do
                                   begin
                                   Gonext;
                                   bufpos:=Succ(bufpos);
                                   end

else
{deletion and restart}
if keycode = 'ESC' then begin
                           GotoXY(x_begin,y_begin);
                           bufpos:=0;
                           StringBuffer:='';
                           end;
end;

CsrOff;
xpos:=WhereX;ypos:=WhereY;     {stores current position}
GotoXY(x_begin,y_begin);       {starting position}
```

```
for i:=1 to Length (stringbuffer) do {writes the new
                                          string}
begin
    WriteAttribute(0,stringbuffer[i],attribute);
    GoNext;
end;

while not (WhereX >= x_begin + size)
    and not (WhereX = colnum)
                              do write (' ');

GotoXY(xpos,ypos);         {end of zone filled with spaces}
                           {but only on screen:}
                           {buffer unchanged}
CsrOn;

until keycode = 'ENT';     {end of input}

Move(StringBuffer,str,Length(StringBuffer)+1);
     {+1 for StringBuffer[0] = length}
end;
```

declarations: GetScreen, CsrOff, CsrOn, WriteAttribute, KbdStat, Inkey.

NOTES:

During editing, all positions not occupied by the buffer and up to the maximum length allowed by buffer are set to space and therefore delete the corresponding location on the screen (see above).

Editing a string that extends over two lines is not possible.

Since procedure Read is not used, variable BufLen is not reinitialized to 127 between each read. It is therefore unnecessary to reassign it between each call to InputString.

If you want to change the appearance of the cursor during editing, add supplementary parameters to the procedure and insert procedure SetCursor from the chapter on display at the right point.

NB:

The processing time for each character is not negligible, so it is better to compile the program with the C switch set to {$C–} to avoid losing characters being typed ahead.

restrictions on use: None.

3.6 Procedure InputReal and InputInt

It would be a pity to limit the ease of input provided by InputString to string characters alone. Here then are two procedures allowing you to input an integer or a real number under the same conditions.

syntax: InputReal (r,attribute);
InputInt (i,attribute);

r is of real type, i is of integer type, attribute is of byte type.

function:

Reading an integer or a real number under the same conditions as those described in InputString.

A supplementary functionality illustrates the procedures described in the chapter on the screen display: if one of the characters input cannot be converted to a number, the string is redisplayed showing the first character causing the error in reverse video mode.

mechanism:

We use procedure InputString to enter the character string representing the number. Next we simply have to call the standard val procedure to convert this string to a number.

If this conversion leads to an error, the incorrect character is displayed in reverse video and input starts again from scratch.

listing:

```
procedure InputReal(var variable:real;attribute:byte);

var
    buffer          :     linestring;
    keepx,keepy     :     byte;
    code            :     integer;

begin
    keepx:=WhereX;keepy:=WhereY;  {start of input position}
    repeat
    GotoXY(keepx,keepy);
    InputString(buffer,attribute);
    Var(buffer,variable,code);     {input valid?}
    if not (code = 0) then     begin
                               GotoXY(keepx,keepy);
                               write(buffer);
    {not indispensable}        GotoXY(keepx,keepy);
                               write(buffer);
    {not indispensable}        GotoXY(keepx+code-1,keepy);
                                   {erroneous character}
                                   {and modifiable}
                               Invert(GetBackGround);
                                   {highlighted}
                               end;
    until code = 0;
    end;

    procedure InputInt(var variable:integer;attribute:byte);
```

```
    {as above but untyped variables}
    {are not accepted here}

    var
         buffer            :    linestring;
    keepx,keepy            :    byte;
         code              :    integer;

begin
    keepx:=WhereX;keepy:=WhereY;
    repeat
    GotoXY(keepx,keepy);
    InputString(buffer,attribute);
    Val(buffer,variable,code);
    if not (code = 0) then begin
    GotoXY(keepx,keepy);
    write(buffer);
    GotoXY(keepx+code-1,keepy);
    Invert(GetBackGround);
    end;

    until code = 0;

end;
```

declarations: GetDisplay, CsrOn, CsrOff, WriteAttribute, KbdStat, Inkey, InputString, Invert, GetBackGround.

NOTES: None.

restrictions on use: None.

CHAPTER 10

Miscellaneous procedures and functions

1 AIMS OF THE CHAPTER

The procedures and functions discussed in this chapter cover fields that are too restricted to have a whole chapter to themselves. Nevertheless, they are useful additions to the library already built up through the first nine chapters.

These routines will generally be declarable on their own and will cover the following fields:

—system time management

—extended memory functions to supplement functions MemAvail and MaxAvail

—mathematic functions

—management of program parameters entered under DOS (for those who do not have version 3.0 of Turbo Pascal)

—procedures bsave and bload

—reading the DOS version

—the musical utility.

2 PROCEDURES AND FUNCTIONS

2.1 System time and date management

The time and date are important parameters in many applications. It is therefore necessary to have a minimum number of routines allowing the system time and date to be read from within the programs, to modify them and to display them simply in a standard format.

2.1.1 Procedure GetDate

syntax: GetDate;

function:

Returns the elements of the system date in the following variable globals:

—DosDay
—DosMonth
—DosYear.

These global variables are of integer type.

pseudo-code:

a. load the service number 42 into AH
b. call the DOS interrupt
c. read the day from DL
d. the month from DH
e. and the year from CX.

mechanism:

Simple DOS call.

listing:

```
var
    DosDay, DosMonth, DosYear:integer;

procedure GetDate;

type
    result = record
               AX,BX,CX,DX,BP,SI,DI,DS,ES,flags:integer;
             end;

var
    params: result;

begin
    params.AX:=$2A00;              {function $2A}
    MsDos(params);
    DosDay:=Lo(params.DX);         {day in DL}
    DosMonth:=Hi(params.DX);       {month in DH}
    DosYear:=params.CX;            {year in CX}
end;
```

NOTES: None.

restrictions on use: None.

2.1.2 Function Date

This function allows you to obtain the system date in a simple way when editing on screen or printer.

syntax: Date;

the value returned is of the date_string type = string [10].

function:

Returns the date in the form dd/mm/yyyy.

pseudo-code:

a. call GetDate
b. convert DosDay, DosMonth and DosYear into character strings.

listing:

```
type  date_string = string[10];

function Date:date_string;

var
    day, month      :     string[2];
         year       :     string[4];

begin

GetDate;
Str(DosDay:2,day);
if DosDay  then day[1]:='0';

Str(DosMonth:2,month);
if DosMonth then month[1]:='0';

Str(DosYear:4,year);
Date:=day+'/'+month+'/'+year;

end;
```

declarations: GetDate.

NOTES: None.

restrictions on use: None.

2.1.3 Procedure SetDate

SetDate is an indispensable supplement to the previous procedures, allowing you to update the system date from within your programs.

syntax: SetDate (day, month, year);

all parameters are of the integer type.

function:

Updates the system date from the parameters passed. To ensure that the parameters entered are consistent with system requirements, the global variable DateOk is updated and is set to true if the operation is successful.

pseudo-code:

a. load service number 43 into AH
b. load the month into DH and the day into DL

c. load the year into CX
d. call DOS
e. read the return code in AL.

mechanism:

Simple DOS call

listing:

```
var DateOk      :    boolean;

procedure SetDate (day, month, year: integer);

type
    result = record
               AX,BX,CX,DX,BP,SI,DI,DS,ES,flags:integer;
             end;

var
    params     : result;

begin
   params.AX:=$2B00;          {function $2B}
   params.DX:=month SHL 8 or day;
   params.CX:=year;
   MsDos(params);
   DateOk:=(Lo(params.AX) = 0);
end;
```

declarations: None.

NOTES:

If one of the parameters is incorrect, AL will contain FFH on exit from the procedure.

restrictions on use: None.

Procedures GetTime and SetTime and Function Time are strictly equivalent, at the level of the mechanism used, to the procedures and functions concerning the date.

The difference is at the level of the function numbers and the contents of registers:

—GetTime : DOS function 44
—SetTime : DOS function 45
—the hour is read from or passed through CH
—the minutes are passed through or read from CL
—seconds are passed through or read from DH, and it is even possible to read hundredths of a second from DL.

2.1.4 Procedure GetTime

syntax: GetTime;

function:

Returns the system time in hours, minutes and seconds in:

—DosHour
—DosMinute
—DosSecond.

listing:

```
var
    DosHour, DosMinute, DosSecond:integer;

procedure GetTime;

type
    result = record
              AX,BX,CX,DX,BP,SI,DI,DS,ES,flags:integer;
             end;

var
    params:   result;

begin
    params.AX:=$2C00;                {function $2C}
    MsDos(params);
    DosHour:=Hi(params.CX);          {hours in CH}
    DosMinute:=Lo(params.CX);        {minutes in CL}
    DosSecond:=Hi(params.DX);        {seconds in DH}
end;
```

declarations: None.

NOTES: None.

2.1.5 Function Time

syntax: Time;

function:

Returns the system time in the form hh/mm/ss/

listing:

```
type time_string = string[8];

function Time:time_string;

var
    hour, minute, second: string[2];

begin
```

```
GetTime;
Str(DosHour:2,hour); if DosHour  then hour [1]:= '0';
Str(DosMinute:2,minute); if DosMinute  then minute[1]:='0';
Str(DosSecond:2,second); if DosSecond  then second[1]:='0';
Time:=hour+':'+minute+':'+second;
end;
```

declarations: None.

NOTES: None.

restrictions on use: None.

2.1.6 Procedure SetTime

syntax: SetTime (hours,minutes, seconds);

all parameters are of integer type.

function:
Updates the system time using the values of the parameters passed.

listing:

```
var TimeOk:boolean;

procedure SetTime(hour,minute,second:integer);

type
    result = record
               AX,BX,CX,DX,BP,SI,DI,DS,ES,flags:integer;
             end;

var
    params: result;

begin
    params.AX:=$2D00;
    params.CX:=hour shl 8 or minute;
    params.DX:=second shl 8;
    MsDos(params);
    TimeOk:=(Lo(params.AX))=0;      {AL = 0 if no error}
end;
```

declarations: None.

NOTES: None.

restrictions on use: None.

2.2 Functions concerning memory

2.2.1 Function TotMemAmount

It is often important for an application to know the total amount of memory available in the system. This value is provided by interrupt 12H.

syntax: TotMemAmount;

the value returned is of the integer type.

function:

Returns the total quantity of memory installed on the system in KBytes.

mechanism:

Call to interrupt 12H and reading of 1K blocks in AX.

listing:

```
function TotMemAmount:integer;

type
      result  = record
                 AX,BX,CX,DX,BP,SI,DI,DS,ES,flags:integer;
                end;

var
     params: result;

begin
     intr($12,params);
     TotMemAmount:=params.AX;        {number of 1K blocks}
end;
```

declarations: None.

NOTES:

The value returned is not calculated but based on the positions of DIP switches installed on the main board. If they are incorrectly positioned, the value returned will obviously be wrong.

restrictions on use: None.

2.2.2 Function FreeMemAmount

syntax: FreeMemAmount;

the value returned is of the integer type (in Kbytes).

function:

Returns the amount of memory left free by the program.

pseudo-code:

a. load function number 72 into AH
b. saturate BX
c. call DOS
d. read the number of free paragraphs in BX.

mechanism:

DOS function 72 is in fact a memory space allocation function. The trick is to ask the system for more memory than it can allocate. The system then returns the maximum number of paragraphs available in BX. A paragraph represents 16 bytes, so we simply have to divide the number by 64 to obtain the number of Kbytes available.

listing:

```
function FreeMemAmount:integer;

type
    result = record
              AX,BX,CX,DX,BP,SI,DI,DS,ES,flags:integer;
             end;

var
    params : result;

begin

with params do
begin
AX:=$4800;
BX:=$FFFF;            {absurd request for allocation of 1 Mbyte}
MsDos(params);
FreeMemAmount:=BX div 64;      {system response: 'BX'
                                available}
                               {amount given in 16-byte
                                paragraphs}

end;
end;
```

declarations: None.

NOTES:

Note that if no precise instruction concerning limitation to the stack segment is given on compilation, the value returned by this function will always be zero as Turbo Pascal automatically allocates all available memory for stack and heap management. We shall return to this point in our user hints.

restrictions on use: None.

2.3 Mathematic functions

What follows is a fairly complete collection of mathematic functions that are not available in the standard system. Include them once and for all in a file that you can compile with your program every time your applications have to carry out any unusual calculations.

Since the value of these functions is purely mathematical and their coding is always simple, we shall simply describe their functions.

List of functions:

ExpReal(a,x) : raising a real number to a real power
ExpInt (a,x) : raising an integer to an integer power
ConvRad (angle) : conversion of an angular measure from degree to radians
DegToDec : converts a string representing degrees, minutes and seconds of angle into a decimal value:

1, 2 or 3 first characters: degrees (followed by a [degree sign])

1 or 2 further characters: minutes (followed by a ^)

(to avoid confusion with ')

final 1 or 2 characters: seconds (followed by ")

DecToDeg : inverse function of the preceding one (but the sign ^ is replaced by a ')

ArcSin (sin) : returns the Arcsine of the specified sine

ArcCos (cos) : returns the Arccosine of the specified cosine

Tan (angle) : tangent of an angle expressed in radians

SinH (x)

CosH (x)

TanH (x) : hyperbolic sine, cosine and tangent of a real number

ArcSinH (sinh)

ArcCosH (cosh)

ArcTanH (tanh) : inverse functions of the preceding ones

Log (base,r) : returns the logarithm to any base of a real number

Fact (n) : returns the factorial of an integer up to 33

Hex (n) : converts an integer to a hexadecimal string

Dec ('hhhh') : inverse funtion of preceding one (returns 0 in case of error)

listing:

```
function ExpReal(a,x:real):real;

begin ExpReal:=Exp(x*Ln(a)); end;

function ExpInt(a,x:integer):integer;

var
    a_real,x_real:real;

begin
a_real:=int(a);x_real:=int(x);
ExpInt:=Round(Exp(x_real*Ln(a_real)));
end;

function ConvRad(angle:real):real;

begin
ConvRad :=Pi * angle / 180;
end;

function ConvDeg(angle:real):real;

begin
ConvDeg := 180 * angle / Pi;
end;

type angle = string[10];

function DegToDec(str:angle):real;

var
    code,degrees,minutes,seconds:integer;

begin

    if Length(str) in [9..10] then
    begin

    Val(Copy(str,1,2+length(str)-9),degrees,code);
    Val(Copy(str,Pos('#',str)+1,Pos('^',str)-Pos('#',str)-1),
                                             minutes,code);
    Val(Copy(str,Pos('^',str)+1,Pos(''',str)-Pos('^',str)-1),
                                             seconds,code);
    if code=0 then DegToDec:=degrees+minutes/60+seconds/3600;
    end;

end;
```

```
function DecToDeg(val:real):angle;

var
           buffer1     :    string[3];
buffer2,buffer3     :    string[2];

begin

    Str(Trunc(val):3,buffer1);

    Str(Round(Frac(val)*60):2,buffer2);
    if buffer2[1]=' ' then buffer2[1]:='0';

    Str (Round(Frac(Frac(val)*60)*60):2,buffer3);
    if buffer3[1]=' ' then buffer3[1]:='0';

DecToDeg:=buffer1+'''+buffer2+''''+buffer3''';

end;

function ArcSin(sin:real):real;

begin
    if (sin >= -1) and (sin <=1) then
              ArcSin:=ArcTan(sin/Sqrt(1-Sqr(sin)));
end;

function ArcCos(cos:real):real;

begin
if (cos >=1) and (cos <=1) then
              ArcCos:=1.570796-ArcTan(cos/Sqrt(1-Sqr(cos)));

end;

function Tan(angle:real):real;

begin
Tan:=sin(angle);
end;

function SinH(x:real):real;

begin
SinH:=(Exp(x)-Exp(-x))/2;
end;

function CosH(x:real):real;
```

```
begin
CosH:=(Exp (x) + Exp (-x)) /2;
end;

function TanH (x:real): real;

begin
TanH:=SinH(x)/CosH(x);
end;

function ArcSinH(x:real):real;

begin
ArcSinH:=Ln(x+Sqrt(Sqr(x)+1));
end;

function ArcCosH(x:real):real;

begin
if x >= 1 then
ArcCosH:=Ln(x+Sqrt(Sqr(x)-1));
end;

function ArcTanH(x:real):real;

begin
if (x >= -1) and (x <= 1) then
ArcTanH:=Ln((1+x)/(1-x))/2;
end;

Type code_hexa = string[4];

function hex(n:integer):code_hexa;

type byte_hexa = string[2];

function convert(m:byte):byte_hexa;       {conversion
                                           sub-function}

const
    digits:string[16] = '0123456789ABCDEF';

var
    digit1,digit2: char;

begin
    digit1:=digits[m div 16+1];
    digit2:=digits[m+1-(m div 16)*16];
```

```
    convert:=digit1+digit2;
end;

begin
    hex:=convert(Hi (n)) + convert (Lo(n));
end;

function dec (word_hexa:code_hexa):integer;

const digits:string[16] = '0123456789ABCDEF';

var
    i,buffer  :  integer;
         ok   :  boolean;

begin

for i:=1 to 4 do ok:= Upcase(word_hexa[i]) in ['A'..'F','0'..
                                                          '9'];
     {valid characters?}

if (Length(word_hexa) <4) or not ok
then
dec:= 0
else
begin
buffer:=0;
for i:= 1 to 4 do
    buffer:=buffer+(Pos(Upcase(word_hexa[i],digits)-1)
              * ExpInt(16,4-i);
    dec:=buffer;
    end;                 {remember to declare ExpInt}

end;

function Fact(n:integer):integer;

begin
    if n=0 then Fact:=1 else Fact := n * Fact(n-1);
end;
```

2.4 Procedure Params

Though version 3.0 has corrected the oversight, the earlier versions of Turbo Pascal did not allow recovery of parameters entered on the DOS command line when the program was launched, which limited possibilities for parameter passing and therefore limited the potential of applications. We wrote this procedure for version 2.0, and include it here for those who do not yet have the later version. Readers who already have the more advanced system should still benefit from the examination we give of the parameter passing mechanism.

syntax: Params;

function:

Returns parameters entered on the command line which launched the program, in global variable params, and the number of those parameters in global variable NbParams.

Params is of type param = array [1...10] of string [20]. NbParams is of the byte type.

Array Params contains parameters entered on the DOS command line and separated by slashes. NbParams contains the number of parameters entered.

Parameters must contain no more than 20 characters and the total number of parameters cannot be greater than 10.

These limitations can be modified, but it must be borne in mind that the PSP can only handle a total of 127 characters in parameters (the PSP is the program segment prefix created by DOS each time a program is launched).

The area beginning at offset 80H of the PSP contains the whole character string passed on the command line. It later becomes the DTA by default. (See the explanations given in the chapter on floppy disks.)

All spaces within the string are eliminated.

This procedure is already included in version 3.0 of Turbo Pascal.

Its value is therefore only educational, unless you want separators to be something other than spaces or if you have an earlier version of the system.

E.g.:

If, under DOS, you have launched a test program, try typing the command:

A>test parameter1/parameter2

NbParams will contain the value 2
Params[1] will take the value 'parameter1'
Params[2] will take the value 'parameter2'.

pseudo-code:

For procedure ParseCommand see the chapter on the printer where we used this procedure for the first time.

a. eliminate spaces
b. while the length of the chain is non-zero
   b1. increment the number of parameters
   b2. call ParseCommand
   b3. store the parameter in Params.

mechanism:

See our explanation of the PSP. The most important thing is to define an absolute address variable at offset 80H of the code segement.

listing:

```
type
    parm = array[1..10] of string[20];

var
    Parms    :    parm;
  NbParms    :    byte;

procedure Params;

type
    psp_zone = string[127];
 parmsbuffer = string[20];

var
Parms_Zone :  psp_zone absolute Cseg:$80; {Program
                                           Segment Prefix}
buffer     :  parmsbuffer;

procedure ParseCommand(var command:psp_zone;var
buffer:parmsbuffer);

{comments already included in chapter on printer}

begin
    if Pos('/',command)=0
    then
    begin
    buffer:=Copy(command,1,20);
    command:='';
    end
    else
    begin
    buffer:=Copy(command,1,Pos('/',command)-1);
    Delete(command,1,Pos('/',command));
    end;
end;

begin

    while Pos(' ',Parms_Zone)0 do
        delete(Parms_Zone,Pos(' ',Parms_Zone),1);
    {eliminate spaces}
    NbParms:=0;
```

```
    while not(Length(Parms_Zone)=0) do
    begin

    NbParms:=Succ(Nbparms);                    {another parameter}
    ParseCommand(Parms_Zone,buffer);           {extraction from
                                                the PSP storage}
    Parms[NbPrams]:=buffer;
    end;

end;
```

restrictions on use: None.

2.5 Memory image files / BSave and BLoad

The storage of a file in a specific part of memory in order to reload it subsequently by an inverse procedure may be necessary in certain types of application, of which the most common example is the storage of screen images (see the chapter on graphics). We shall consider a set of two procedures allowing a disk file to be saved in any part of system memory and its restoration later at an address which may be different from its source address.

On the other hand, you may need to load or save memory image files which were created in BASIC or which you want to be able to use in the IBM PC's BASIC. We suggest two further procedures which allow a Turbo Pascal program to load a file created by the BASIC BSave instruction, and which will allow a Turbo Pascal program to generate a file which can be accessed by using BASIC's BLoad instruction.

The constraints on formating of these files to make them compatible with BASIC have lead us to handle data transfer byte by byte. The two procedures are therefore far slower than those above and can only be used for these specific purposes.

NOTES:

Procedures BLoad and BLoadBas will produce no effect if the file to load does not exist. It is up to the reader to add the necessary code for handling such an error.

2.5.1 Procedure BSave

syntax: BSave (segment, offset, length, userfile);

segment, offset and length are of the integer type, userfile is of the filespec type = string [40].

function:

Saves the memory zone starting at address segement : offset in the file specified by user files.

Length defines the number of bytes to save starting from that origin.

pseudo-code:

a. initialize the file

b. while the length to save is greater than 128 bytes
   b1. load 128 bytes from the memory zone into the buffer
   b2. write them to a file
   b3. reduce the value of length by 128

c. if there are less than 128 bytes remaining
   c1. initialize the buffer to zero
   c2. load the remaining bytes into it
   c3. write them to the file

d. close the file.

mechanism:

The use of BlockWrite (and later BlockRead) allows very rapid disk read and write procedures to be developed.

Section c, which deals with the end of the block to save, makes it possible to avoid writing parasite data to the file, as would happen if a full 128-block was written with no special precautions.

listing:

```
procedure
BSave(segment,offset,length:integer;userfile:filespec);


var
    binfile   : FILE;
      index   : integer;
     buffer   : array[0..127] of byte;


begin


    assign(binfile,userfile);
    rewrite(binfile);


    index:=0;


while not (length <128) do    {writing full blocks}
begin


    Move(Mem[segment:offset+index*128],buffer,128);
    BlockWrite(binfile,buffer,1);
    index:=index+1;
    length:=length-128;        {another full block?}
end;
```

```
if not (length=0) then          {final group of bytes}
begin

    FillChar(buffer,SizeOf(buffer),0);
    Move(mem[segment:offset+index*128],buffer,length);
    BlockWrite(binfile,buffer,1);
end;

close(binfile);

end;
```

declarations: None.

NOTES:

Memory screen handling is possible. However, reading and writing to this memory in colour text mode produces a snowstorm effect, so it is more elegant to top and tail the data transfer with procedures switch_display_off and switch_display_on to 'turn off' the screen and avoid these unpleasent parasite effects.

The format used, without a header, is not compatible with files created by instruction BSave in BASIC. (See later for compatible procedures.)

restrictions on use: None.

2.5.2 Procedure BLoad

This procedure is the inverse of the previous one.

syntax: BLoad (segment, offset, length, userfile);

the parameters are of the same type as above.

function:

Restores a number of bytes equal to length from the contents of file userfile to the memory address specified by segement: offset.

mechanism:

Exactly the inverse of procedure BSave.

listing:

```
procedure
BLoad(segment,offset,length:integer;userfile:filespec);

var
    binfile   : file;
      index   : integer;
     buffer   : array[0..127] of byte;
```

```
begin

     {$I-}
     assign(binfile,userfile);
     reset(binfile);
     {$I+}
     if IOresult = 0 then      {the file exists}

begin
index:=0;
while not (length<128) do      {as for BSave}
begin
    BlockRead(binfile,buffer,1);
    Move(buffer,Mem[segment:offset+index*128],1280;
    index:=index+1;
    length:=length-128;
end;

if not (length=0) then
begin
     BlockRead(binfile,buffer,1);
     Move(buffer,Mem[segment:offset+index*128],length);
end;

close(binfile);

end;
```

declarations: None.

NOTES:

Take care in choosing load addresses.
The same comments apply as for BSave concerning compatibility.

restrictions on use: None.

2.5.3 Procedures BSaveBas and BLoadBas

As we said above, it can be useful to read into Turbo Pascal's files created by BASIC (e.g. screen images created by a graphics program). The inverse may also be true.

In this case, it is necessary to conform to the specifications of BLoad and BSave files in BASIC. The conventions are:

—the first byte in the file always contains $FD

—bytes 2 and 3 contain the segment number with the less significant byte first

—bytes 4 and 5 : the same for the offset

—bytes 6 and 7 : the same for the length— the actual data begin at byte 8

—the end of file is marked by $1A.

We therefore simply have to reproduce this structure. But such a structure has one major disadvantage in that it shifts all data by 7 bytes, preventing our use of a simple block by block process (it would perhaps be possible for saving, but reading of data in this way would be impossible—at least in any simple way). We therefore work byte by byte, which makes transfer time longer. This is not a very serious problem given that this kind of processing is unlikely to be used very often.

Procedure BSaveBas

syntax: BSaveBas (segment, offset, length, userfile);

same types of parameters as BLoad and BSave.

function:

Saves the contents of memory specified by address segement:offset, for a number of bytes equal to length, in a file in BASIC format.

pseudo-code:

a. initialize the file
b. generate a 'header' using the parameters passed
c. write the memory zone byte by byte
d. write the end of file marker.

mechanism:

Note the inversion of the less significant and more significant bytes in each parameter.

listing:

```
procedure BSaveBas(segment,offset,length:integer;userfile:
filespec);

var
    binfile    :  file of byte;
          i    :  integer;
fbyte,mark     :  byte;
begin

assign(binfile,userfile);
rewrite(binfile);

mark:=$FD;write(binfile,mark);      {reconstitute the header}
mark:=Lo(segment);write(binfile,mark);
mark:=Hi(segment);write(binfile,mark);
mark:=Lo(offset);write(binfile,mark);
mark:=Hi(offset);write(binfile,mark);
```

```
mark:=Lo(length);write(binfile,mark);
mark:=Hi(length);write(binfile,mark);

for i:=1 to length do write (binfile,Mem[segment:
                                 offset+i-1]);
mark:=$1A;                       {end of file}
write(binfile,mark);

close(binfile);

end;
```

declarations: None.

NOTES: None.

restrictions on use:

Use only to deal with compatibility problems.

Procedure BLoadBas

syntax: BLoadBas (userfile);

userfile is of the filespec type.

function:

Restores to memory an image saved under BASIC, using instruction BSave, to the original address.

pseudo-code:

a. initialize the file
b recalculate the segment, offset and address
c. load the memory image byte by byte.

listing:

```
procedure BLoadBas(userfile:filespec);

var
                binfile :  file of byte;
segment,offset,length,i :  integer;
                 fbyte  :  byte;

begin

    {$i-}
    assign(binfile,userfile);
    reset(binfile);
    {$I+}
    if IOresult = 0 then      {the file exists}
```

```
    begin
    read(binfile,fbyte);
    if fbyte = $FD then       {A Basic BSave file}
    begin

    read(binfile,fbyte);segment:=fbyte; {calculation
                                          of address}
    read(binfile,fbyte);segment:=segment+fbyte*256;
    read(binfile,fbyte);offset:=fbyte;
    read(binfile,fbyte);offset:=offset+fbyte*256;
    read(binfile,fbyte);length:=fbyte;
    read(binfile,fbyte);length:=length+fbyte*256;

    for i:=1 to length do
    read(binfile,Mem[segment:offset+i-1]);
    end;

    close(binfile);
    end;
end;
```

declarations: None.

NOTES: None.

Loading takes place automatically at the same address and on the same length as specified during saving under BASIC.

If this is a problem, a procedure will need to be written for passing the segment, offset and length required. The first seven bytes, which are then unnecessary, would have to be dropped.

restrictions on use: As for BSaveBas.

2.6 Function DosVersion

To ensure compatibility between systems, your programs will need to know the DOS version number under which they run.

This function will return the information with no difficulty.

syntax: DosVersion;

the value returned is of version type = string [5].

function:

Returns a string, of five characters at most, indicating the current DOS version you are running.

pseudo-code:

a. load function number 48 into AH
b. call DOS

c. if AL = zero the version is lower than 2.0
d. otherwise AL = prefix and AH = suffix.

mechanism:

Simple DOS call.

listing:

```
type version =string[5];

function DosVersion:version;

type

    result = record
              AX,BX,CX,DX,BP,SI,DI,DS,ES,flags:integer;
             end;

var
    params      : result;
major,minor     : string[2];

begin

with params do
begin
AX:=$3000;               {function $30}
MsDos(params);
if Lo(AX)=0 then
              DosVersion:='1.xx'  {version number less
                                   than 2.0}
              else

              begin
              Str(Lo(AX),major);Str(Hi(AX),minor);
              DosVersion:=major+'.'+minor;
              end;
    end;

end;
```

declarations: None.

NOTES: None.

restrictions on use: None.

2.7 Procedure PlayString

To end this chapter on a less serious 'note', we shall propose a procedure here to make the system play a piece of music on the basis of a score you have specified for it.

syntax: PlayString (tempo,style,str);

tempo is of the integer type, style is of the musicstyle type = (n,1,s), str is of the played_string type = string [252].

function:

Executes the piece of music specified by str using the following conventions:

Parameter tempo indicates the base duration of notes in milliseconds.

Parameter style indicates whether the piece is to be played:

normally (n) duration = duration indicated * 7/8
legato (l) duration = duration indicated * 1
staccato (s) duration = duration indicated * 3/4

The character string has the following structure:

Each note to play is represented by an incompressible group of six characters.

For each note, the first character represents the octave in which the note is to be played. The value can vary from 1 to 6. It only applies to the note being considered.

PAU represents a pause and starts with the first character.

The second and third characters represent the note with the following code:

DO D# RE R# MI FA F# SO S# LA L# SI

Lower case may be used.

The fourth and fifth characters represent the factor applied to the base duration.

Depending on whether the 6th character is +, ., – or :, the result will be:

+ the base duration is multiplied by the value indicated
. the base duration is multiplied by the value indicated * 3/2
– the base duration is divided by the value indicated
: the base duration is divided by the value indicated * 3/2

This makes it easy to translate scores and to establish equivalence between the duration of notes and the duration of the sound.

E.g.: if the base duration is a crotchet

02+ is a minim
02– is a quaver
04– is a semi-quaver
02: is a dotted quaver
01. is a dotted crotchet, etc.

The same applies to pauses. The multiplication factor can vary from 00 to 99 and must contain two digits.

E.g.:

3DO03+ plays a DO in the 3rd octave
duration = base duration*3
6F#02. plays F sharp in the 6th octave
duration = base duration*2*3/2
1S104– plays a first octave B
duration = base duration divided by div 4

The maximum number of notes is 42, but it is not difficult, using several PlayString instructions together, to make up quite long pieces.

pseudo-code:

Procedure Play

a. establish the base frequency at 32 625
b. multiply this frequency by two as often as needed to reach the specified octave
c. find the position of the note requested in the scale and multiply the basic frequency by 1.059463094 as often as necessary to reach the note required (1.059463094 represents the frequency ratio between two notes in the scale)
d. trigger the loudspeaker at the calculator frequency and for the specified duration.

body of the procedure:

a. determine the style factor
b. for each group of 6 characters in str...
c. find the octave, note, duration and multiplying factor(mode)
d. call Play, passing these parameters to it.

listing:

```
type
    played_string = string[252];
       musicstyle = (n,l,s);

procedure
PlayString(temp:integer;style:musicstyle;str:
                                                  played_string);

type
    name_note = string[2];

var
           stylefactor    :  real;
octave,duration,code,i    :  integer;
                  note    :  name_note;
                  mode    :  char;
procedure Play(octave,duration:integer;note:name_note);


const game:string[24]='DOD#RER#'MIFAF#SOS#LAL#SI';
```

```
var
        frequency :    real
        i, level  :    integer;

begin

    frequency:=32.625;          {base frequency}
    for I := 1 to octave do
    frequency:=frequency * 2; {frequency of the octave}

for I: 0 to ((Pos(note,scale)+1) div 2)-1 do
frequency:=frequency * 1.059463094;
                                         {note frequency}

if duration <> 0 then

begin

    sound(Round(frequency));
    delay(Round(duration*stylefactor));
    nosound;
    delay(Round(duration*(1-stylefactor)));{length of
                              {time associated with style}
    end;

end;

begin

    case style of
    n     : stylefactor:=7/8;       {normal}
    l     : stylefactor:=1;         {legato}
    s     : stylefactor:=3/4;       {staccato}
    end;

if (Length(str) mod 6 = 0) then     {valid string?}

begin

for i:=1 to (Length(str) do str[i]:=Upcase(str[i]);

for i:=0 to (Length(str) div 6)-1 do    {for each group}
                                       {of six characters}
begin
Val(Copy(str,i*6+1,1),octave,code);  {calculate octave}
if octave <1 then octave:=1;
if octave >6 then octave:=6;

note:=Copy(str,i*6+2,2);            {calculate duration}
```

```
Val(Copy(str,i*6+4,2),duration,code); {calculate
                                        duration}

mode:=Copy(str,i*6+6,1);                {and its style}

case mode of

'+'  :    duration:=Round(tempo * duration);
'.'  :    duration:=Round(tempo * duration * 3/2);
'-'  :    duration:=Round(tempo div duration);
':'  :    duration:=Round(tempo div duration * 3/2);

end;

if not (note='AU')  {the P in PAU is simply filling}
    then
    Play(octave,duration,note)
    else
    delay(duration);

    end; {end of note}
    end; {end of string}

end;
```

declarations: None.

NOTES:

Below we give some examples of scores that can be immediately used. It is up to you to write others.

listing:

```
GOD SAVE THE QUEEN

'3SO01+3SO01+3LA01+3F#01.3SO02-3LA01+3SI01+3SI01+4DO01+3SI01.
3LA02-'+
'3SO01+3LA01+3SO01+3F#01+3SO02.4RE01+4RE01+4RE01+4RE01.4DO02-3
SI01+'+
'4dO01+4DO01+4DO01+4DO01.3SI02-3LA01+3SI01+4DO02-3S102-3LA02-3
SO02-'+
'3SI01.4DO02-4RE01+4MI02-4DO02-3SI01+3LA01+3SO02.'


THEME FROM BEETHOVEN'S NINTH

1st phrase
'3SI01+3SI01+4DO01+4RE01+4RE01+4DO01+3SI01+3LA01+3SO01+3SO01+3
LA01+'+
```

```
'3SI01+3SI01.3LA02-3LA02+3SI01+3SI01+4DO01+4RE01+4RE01+4DO01+
 18I01+'+
'3LA01+3SO01+3SO01+3LA03+3SI01+3LA01.3SO02-3SO02+'

second phrase
'3LA01+3LA01+3SI01+3SO01+3LA01+3SI02-4DO02-3SI01+3SO01+3LA01+
 3SI02-'+
'4DO02-3SI01+3SO01+3LA01+3SI02-4DO02-3SI01+3LA01+3SO01+3LA01+
 3RE01+'+
'3SI02+3SI01+4DO01+4RE01+4RE01+4DO01+3SI01+4DO02-3LA02-3SO01+
 3SO01+'+
'3LA01+3SI01+3LA01.3SO02-3SO02+'


OH! SUSANNA

1st phrase
'3SO04-3LA04-3SI02-4RE02-4RE02-4MI02-4RE02-3SI02-3SO02:3LA04-
 3SI02-3SI02-'+
'3LA02-3SO02-3LA01.3SO04-3LA04-3SI02-4RE02-4RE02-4MI02-4RE02-
 3SI02-3SO02:'+
'3LA04-3SI02-3SI02-3LA02-3SO01+PAU01+'

second phrase
'4DO01+4DO01+4MI02-4MI01+4MI02-4RE02-4RE02-3SI02-3SO02-3LA01+
 PAU02-3SO04-'+
'3LA04-3SI02-4RE02-4RE02-4MI02-4RE02-3SI02-3SI02:3LA04-3SIO2-
 3SIO2-3LA02-'+
'3LA02-3SO01+'
```

restrictions on use: None.

Hints and Appendices

1 INSTALLATION OF EDITOR COMMANDS

When installing the Turbo Pascal system on your PC you must have had some problem trying to find more sensible commands than Ctrl-K Ctrl-W or Ctrl-Q Ctrl-P.

Generally, the possibility is provided of selecting your own command characters, but not all are acceptable. After some investigations, we came up with the solutions proposed here.

Clearly, this is a matter of taste and the approach we suggest will not satisfy everybody, but we hope it will be of some assistance.

Cursor Movements:

character left	:	left arrow
character right	:	right arrow
word left	:	Ctrl left arrow
word right	:	Ctrl right arrow
line up	:	up arrow
line down	:	down arrow
scroll up	:	Ctrl T (op)
scroll down	:	Ctrl B (ottom)
page up	:	PgUp
page down	:	PgDn
to left on line	:	F1
to right on line	:	F2
to top of page	:	F3
to bottom of page	:	F4
to top of file	:	F5
to end of file	:	F6
to beginning of block	:	F7
to end of block	:	F8
to last cursor position	:	F9

Insert and delete

insert mode	:	insert
insert line	:	F10
delete line	:	Alt L (ine)
delete to end of line	:	Alt J
delete right word	:	Ctrl X
delete character	:	delete
delete left character	:	backspace

Block commands

mark block begin	:	Alt B (egin)
mark block end	:	Alt F (in)
mark single word	:	Alt G (sinGle)
hide/display block	:	Alt H (ide)
copy block	:	Alt C (opy)
move block	:	Alt M (ove)
delete block	:	Alt D (elete)
read block from disk	:	Alt X (eXternal)
write block to disk	:	Alt Z

Miscellaneous

end edit	:	Alt N (eNd)
tab	:	tab
Auto tab on/off	:	Alt V
restore line	:	Alt K (Alt J, K and L all concerned lines)
find	:	Alt 1
find and replace	:	Alt 2
repeat last find	:	Alt 3
control char.prefix	:	Ctrl P (refix)

Furthermore, certain editor functionalities only begin to appear as we use them and are not mentioned in the documentation.

—if you press the backspace key when the cursor is at the start of a line the current line will be attached to the line before, including any spaces.

—if the insert is active and you press the enter key, the current line will be broken to the right of the cursor and the right-hand part of the line will be inserted between the current line and the following line, taking any indentation options into account.

—again with insert on, if the cursor is at the end of a line, pressing enter will add a new line.

These three functions are very useful and it is generally a good idea to work with insert on.

2 COMPILATION

If you compile your programs with no particular precautions and execute them (in the form of files with the .COM extension generated by Turbo Pascal) under DOS, you will no doubt have noticed that if COMMAND.COM is not on your floppy disk, whenever you exit the program a request always appears to load the file in drive a. Why?

Program COMMAND.COM is installed high up in the system memory. If, during compilation, you do not limit the size of the segment reserved to the stack and the heap, Turbo Pascal automatically assigns them all available memory. In this case, COMMAND.COM will be overwritten and will have to be reloaded when you exit your program.

To avoid this disadvantage the following steps have to be taken:

—compile your program in memory

—at the end of compilation, note down the stack and heap value shown in the summary table as n paragraphs

—enter the Options menu (O)

—go to compilation mode C (.com file)

—enter option A (use maximum free dynamic memory)

—enter the value you found

—exit the options menu and relaunch compilation.

If the value you are shown is such that the location zone for COMMAND.COM is not reached, your program exits will take place without difficulty.

3 INITIALIZATION OF VARIABLES

Unlike other systems (BASIC for example), an unitialized variable in Turbo Pascal does not necessarily have a zero value if it is a numeric variable, and is not necessarily null if it is a string.

Pressing Enter, in response to a read command, does not assign value zero to the variable but leaves it with its current value, i.e. the last value assigned, or an undetermined value.

This is also true when you compile a program in memory, execute it and return to the menu. If you run the program again, the last values assigned to the variables will still be valid. This is, in fact, useful during program development as long as the variable and constant declaration part is not modified.

It is therefore crucial to undertake initialization with care. Two approaches are possible:

—direct assignment within the program

—initialization of a constant with type (and this is the best solution wherever possible).

Remember that constants with types are not real constants but can be simply considered as initialized variables.

4 USER INTERRUPTS

If you want to write your own interrupt routines and call them using instruction Intr, you need a certain amount of information (carefully reread the section on technical generalities).

In the first place, you will need tools allowing you to install an interrupt vector and to check the addresses it contains. This is possible with the following two procedures.

listing:

```
procedure GetVector(vecnumber:integer;var
get_segment,get_offset:integer);
```

```
type
    result = record
              AX,BX,CX,DX,BP,SI,DI,DS,ES,flags:integer;
             end;

var
    params    :    result;

begin

with params do
begin

AX:=$3500 or vecnumber;   {function $ 35}
MsDos(params);
Move(ES,get_segment,2);   {segment in ES}
Move(BX,get_offset,2);    {offset in BX}

end;

end;

var
    saved_segment,saved_offset:integer;

procedure
SetVector(vecnumber,set_segment,set_offset:integer);

type
    result = record
              AX,VX,CX,DX,BP,SI,DI,DS,ES,flags:integer;
             end;

var
    params    :    result;

begin

GetVector(vecnumber,saved_segment,saved_offset);
{save the address of the old routing if there is one}

with params do
begin

AX:=$2500 or vecnumber;   {function $ 25}
move(set_segment,DS,2);   {segment in DS}
Move(set_offset,DX,2);    {offset in DX}
MsDos(params);

end;

end;
```

GetVector uses segment and offset, passed by reference, to return the segment and offset at the start of the interrupt routine whose number is equal to vecnumber.

SetVector replaces the address of the current interrupt routine, whose number is vecnumber, by the address specified by segment: offset. On exit, the global variables saved_segment and saved_offset contain the address of the original routine or zero if the vector was not already occupied.

NB:

You have to use these routines if you want to install an interrupt vector and avoid working directly in memory. Working in memory could have catastrophic effects if the vector concerned had to be used while you were modifying it, and you have no control over this phenomenon.

The value given to vecnumber must normally correspond to a free interrupt number unless you want to replace an existing interrupt. It is impossible to calculate this number inside the program as the value passed to procedure Int and to the assembler instructions must be an immediate value, i.e. a value known on compilation. It is because of this that many resident programs available on the market generate a certain number of compatibility problems since they use the same interrupt number or affect the interrupt used elsewhere.

You therefore need to be extremely careful when installing resident programs, since not all are written with the same care and precautions. We found it impossible to run Turbo Pascal correctly with certain resident programs available commercially, whose names we shall not give, and which are useful in other ways. If you find your Turbo Pascal is behaving abnormally, check first of all that you have not installed some little utility for redefining the keyboard or some other gadget in your autoexec.bat. So, take care!

You can determine empirically which the free vectors are, by using utility DEBUG, provided with the system, to examine the first 256 * 4 bytes in memory. Series of 4 bytes set to zero, starting with an address that is a multiple of 4, represent a free vector. Normally, vectors $60 to $67 are reserved for the user.

It must also be borne in mind that you cannot use standard input/output procedures within an interrupt routine written in Turbo Pascal. This is absolutely illegal and leads to abnormal system behaviour. The consequence is that the possibilities of writing such routines directly in Turbo Pascal are seriously limited, which is a great pity as otherwise it would open up very interesting fields of investigation. Let us hope that it will be possible in the future.

Finally, as specified in your Turbo Pascal documentation, on entry to the interrupt routine the value of DS is incorrect and you therefore no longer have access to global variables, which can be a handicap. The manual's advice on restoring DS is fairly vague. Here is how you should do so:

—declare a constant DataSeg in the principal block as follows:

```
const DataSeg: integer = 0;
```

—before any call to your interrupt routine, execute the following instructions:

```
buffer: = Dseg;
Move (buffer, DataSeg,2);
```

buffer is of integer type.

—just before the first register saving inline instruction in your routine, include the following line:

```
inline ($2E/$1E/DataSeg);
```

From this moment on, you can access global variables in the normal way.

In any case, writing user interrupt routines is only of value if you want to intercept or modify the normal behaviour of system routines and this is difficult to carry out without using the assembler, even if some short range benefits can be obtained using Turbo.

But the development of such techniques would itself merit another book....